PRAIS

The Soul of an Addict

"A must read for both the person who suffers from addiction and those who love the addicts. As a therapist I will be recommending this book to my clients."

–Milt McLelland, CMHC, Roots Counseling Center

"This is one of the best overviews of addiction and recovery from a Christian experiential perspective I have read. It is very readable with examples throughout, and provides a good overview of various approaches to understanding and treating addiction with a fair critique of these. As one who has a doctorate in religion, I find your description of addiction to be realistic, convincing, and very helpful to recognize the god-like power that makes so much sense to the devotee."

–Linford Stutzman, Professor of Religion, Eastern Mennonite University

"The best explanation I've ever read about addiction for the non-addict."

–Ed Marshall, recovering addict

"Your style is lucid and compelling."

–Brendon Walls, Catholic Charities

The Soul of an Addict

UNLOCKING THE COMPLEX NATURE OF SUBSTANCE ADDICTION

D. J. MITCHELL

Published by Alma James Publishing LLC
Harrisonburg, Virginia

www.almajamesbooks.com

www.djmitchellauthor.com

www.thesoulofanaddict.com

I saw a crowd stand talking
I just came up in time
Was teaching the lawyers and the doctors
That a man ain't nothing but his mind...

When Christ taught in the temple
The people all stood amazed
Was teaching the lawyers and the doctors
How to raise a man from the grave

"Soul of a Man"
Blind Willie Johnson
As covered by Bruce Coburn

"If you can't measure it, it doesn't exist."

Saying quoted by Brené Brown

TABLE OF CONTENTS

ACKNOWLEDGMENTS

This book grew out of work on my Capstone Integration Project at Eastern Mennonite Seminary. The Capstone envisioned a healing community in which addicts would meet together frequently and practice Christian discipleship. This book benefited from the wisdom and participation of all who assisted me with that project.

The first draft of the book came together in an amazing six weeks. I am grateful to God for the inspiration. I have never written a draft so quickly!

I am indebted to many people for their help in completing this work. First and foremost is Kent Dunnington, whose book *Addiction and Virtue: Beyond the Models of Disease and Choice* (Downers Grove, IL: Intervarsity Press, 2011) offers the analogy of addiction as "false worship," which provided the framework for much of my analysis. While I don't agree with everything in his book, this analogy opened the door for my work and I am grateful for his insight.

I am greatly indebted to my loving wife, Carrie, without whose support this book would likely have remained unfinished and forgotten. Her patience in listening to multiple drafts borders on saintly, not to mention her tolerance of my spending so much time working at my computer.

My friend Ed Marshall shared his time and experience with me, offering details about his life that most people would have been hesitant to offer for public knowledge. I thank him for his courage, wisdom, and support. He also saved my life many years ago, so without him this book would never have been written.

Russ Eanes edited the manuscript, and I am grateful for his expertise and input. Brendan Walls also offered an in-depth critique. Scott Pollak, who narrated my first novel, *Ordinary World*, suggested the cover design.

Rick Nichols has been generous with his time and wisdom, which I especially appreciate because we do not always see eye to eye. Rick also works with addicts, but from a different perspective. I wish him continued blessings of success.

Many people offered feedback on my various drafts, including Kimberly Lee, Nancy Heisey, Linford Stutzman, Kevin Clark, Anna Efaw, and others. Thank you all.

INTRODUCTION

I am an addict. I've been in recovery for over 35 years. I have not taken a mind-altering drug that was not medically necessary (as determined by a doctor, not myself) since 1985. Nevertheless, I believe that I still have the underlying tendency to abuse drugs or alcohol if I should ever try even social use.

Instead I choose abstinence.

If alcohol or drugs were ruining your life, the logical solution would be to avoid them. Having gotten away from addiction, never touching it again would seem perhaps the only sane response. With so much to lose, why would one take the risk? Yet how often do we see those who have struggled with addiction and gotten clean and sober decide to try the failed experiment of a social drink or drug just one more time? Like touching a hot flame repeatedly, hoping that this time we won't get burned, our reactions seem positively insane.

I've been told that if I'm truly in recovery, or if I've truly accepted Christ, or if I've truly healed, I can take one drink without a problem. But why would I take the risk? That would be crazy.

This is how I know I'm still an addict: even after three decades of being clean, sometimes my brain tries to convince me that just one drink, pill, or fix would be okay. It's that message that convinces me that one of any mind-altering substance will *never* be safe for me.

This book is about addiction. It is written by a recovering addict, and primarily for those who have not experienced addiction. As the rate of deaths from drug overdoses and alcoholism rises, my earnest hope is that it will bring greater understanding to a problem that increasingly affects all segments of the population.

This book seeks to offer practical wisdom, based on decades of observation, into the phenomenon of substance addiction. It is not scientific, and will not discuss neuroscience. I make no claim to being a scientist. It is not medical, because I have at best a passing familiarity with the medical issues. It is not intended to be philosophical, for I am not a philosopher. It is not theological and does not promote a particular religious perspective, though I do have some understanding of theology and am deeply religious myself. It will not make you a substance abuse counselor, nor can it promise that your addicted loved will find recovery. Rather, it seeks to help non-addicts to understand the complex nature of addiction so that they can avoid the temptation of easy answers and simple solutions.

This book considers and draws from multiple theories. It offers, or at least I hope it offers, practical analysis of the problem of addiction that will suggest practical understanding and, ideally, practical responses.

Theories are great. But addiction is the real suffering of real people, families and friends as well as the addicts themselves. Recovery rates among those who identify as addicts (and those whom society has identified as addicts) are well below 50%. Overdose deaths are rising. Deaths from alcohol abuse are rising. If theories don't provide effective solutions, what good are they?

We need answers. We need understanding of the problem. I hope this book helps to move us in that direction.

CHAPTER ONE
THE WHAT AND THE WHY

It seemed like a simple choice: use my paycheck to pay the rent, or to buy drugs. And it *was* a simple choice. Ten years into my addiction, not buying drugs was inconceivable. So I bought drugs. I bought what should have been enough to last a week. But in four hours, it was gone.

I sat there in confusion. How could my life have come to this? Now I had no rent money *and* no drugs. I was in trouble. By the next day, I'd start experiencing withdrawal symptoms. I'd be sick. If I called in sick to work, I wouldn't get paid. Then I'd be in worse shape than ever.

I didn't blame anyone else for my problems. Yes, sometimes I'd rant about my mother, or about the woman I loved who broke up with me. But in moments like these, I knew that it was no one's fault but my own. I was a mess, a walking disaster, and I didn't know how to change.

That was in 1985, when Nancy Reagan was preaching, "Just say no." I'd tried that. I had literally sat on my couch and practiced saying the word "no" over and over, trying to make it a habit. It hadn't worked.

A young Christian woman, the sister of one of my drug suppliers, had tried to save me through church. That hadn't worked, either.

A friend of mine had gotten arrested and sentenced to Twelve Step meetings. She told me, "It's really lame. They sit around and talk about their *feelings*." That didn't sound like it would work for me, either.

I believed that the only way out was death, but I hadn't been able to die. I should have. I'd overdosed five times. I'd driven while too high to see. I'd been in the wrong neighborhoods at the wrong time of night. And I'd put stuff into my body that it was never intended to survive. Yet here I was, sitting at my kitchen table, trying to figure out how to get through another day.

I only knew of one other option: methadone. I called another of my drug suppliers and asked him about it. He was only too happy to steer me to a clinic. From his perspective, once a person gets addicted to methadone, a long-lasting opiate that's hard to quit, it's much more likely they'll return to heroin. I'm sure he didn't have peer-reviewed, double-blind studies to verify that knowledge, but it was true enough for him to steer his customers to a supposed treatment.

But then a strange thing happened. A mutual friend was there, and he asked to speak with me. He explained that methadone is a horrible drug with a withdrawal that lasts for months. The only relief is either more methadone, or heroin. He knew because he was then four months into his own methadone withdrawal.[1] He begged me not to go to the clinic, but to go to a Twelve Step meeting instead.

He offered me hope, and I took it.

I didn't recover right away. For four months I slipped in and out of the program, getting a few days here, a week there, but always returning to drugs and alcohol. I didn't yet grasp what the people at the meetings were trying to tell me. I expected them to teach me how to have willpower. And while I waited, I continued to fail.

Then came the morning I woke up broke again, having spent all my money on drugs the night before. I lay in my bed, miserable, and realized the truth: I couldn't stop. I was hopeless. I was *condemned* to drink and use.

---

[1] His story is told in more detail in the chapter on Addiction Substitution Therapy.

That was my surrender. It *was* the truth—sort of. I couldn't stop drinking and using on my own willpower because my willpower didn't exist in that respect. It wasn't that I was weak. Anyone who can suffer through the misery of the later stages of addiction isn't weak. But I had no willpower when it came to staying off drugs because I didn't believe it was possible. I knew no other way to live.

I crawled back to the Twelve Step meetings, willing to do whatever they said, but still not believing it would work. I did it "one day at a time." I got a sponsor and worked the Steps, expecting at any moment to find myself getting loaded again because that's what I had always done. But the days stretched into weeks, and then months, and I was still clean and sober. I took a six month chip, then a nine month chip, and then a "birthday" cake for a year. As I write this, it has been more than 35 years since that day, and I am still clean and sober.

*   *   *   *

If the decision I made to take drugs rather than pay the rent seems strange to you, even crazy, then this book is written for you. Frankly, that decision makes no sense at all from any conventional, non-addicted perspective. Most people don't understand the thinking of an addict. Even many who suffer from addiction don't really understand why we behave the way we do.

Much has been written about addiction by authors with various perspectives. Science has studied it. Philosophers have considered it. Preachers have preached on it. Yet no single source seems to explain addiction satisfactorily. Each may give us insight, but no single answer gives us the understanding we need to actually *help* those who suffer. I hope that what I've written will help anyone understand addiction better.

The first chapter of this book challenges some of the widely-held myths about addiction, including both the disease model *and* the choice model. Yes, addiction shares some characteristics of disease. Yes, addicts make bad choices. Yet both explanations fail to explain the complexity of characteristics that make addiction so resistant to solutions.

Next I develop the model of addiction as religion, and show how looking at addiction as a false religion offers a useful way of understanding addiction and the elements of a successful approach to recovery. Using anecdotes from my decades of work with addicts and alcoholics, as well as my own story, I explore the characteristics of addiction and what needs these suggest for successful recovery.

The next few chapters consider recovery. I explore the strengths and weaknesses of various approaches, from prison and methadone to Twelve Step programs.

Finally, I explore societal factors that are driving the rise in addiction. From economics and our materialistic national philosophy to a broken mental health care system, there are many reasons people turn to drugs.

Most approaches to recovery don't consider the religious characteristics of addiction, yet these are critically important to understanding it. Let me emphasize once more that I don't deny that addiction is a disease. Rather, I argue that it is *not only* a disease, and approaching it as if it is cannot lead to successful recovery.

I don't deny that addicts make bad choices, and I would never argue that we are not responsible for the consequences of those choices. Our choices are based in an underlying system of belief and morals that can and must change. The

recovered. Sometimes these successes are overlooked in the daily deluge of bad news.

Still, the percentage of people who find recovery remains dismally low. Many recovery programs have success rates under 10%. I believe *we can do better*. And the more we understand addiction, the better equipped we will be to help our struggling friends and loved ones.

CHAPTER TWO
DEFINING ADDICTION

I met Jim in a Twelve Step meeting to which he had come for his heroin addiction. He was in his late twenties, funny, and intelligent. Everyone liked him. He was a talented computer programmer, and had no trouble finding employment. *Keeping* his employment was another matter. Like many addicts, Jim was an unreliable employee.

Jim lived alone in a basement apartment. His landlord, who lived upstairs, did not use drugs. His *environment* was not the cause of his continued drug use. Yet he couldn't seem to quit. He'd been coming to meetings for two years. He'd had several sponsors who had worked the Steps with him, but he had never stopped using drugs for more than a few days. He was desperate, and begged me for help.

This began my two-year relationship with Jim, during which I used everything I had learned in my then more than fifteen years of recovery. But over time, Jim's pattern became clear. He would stop using drugs for three or four days, and then use again.

Heroin withdrawal only lasts a week. I recall more than once telling him, "You're more than half way through. Don't quit now!"

But he never made it to the other side of the withdrawals. He would always use again.

One day, I told him, "You must really like withdrawals. You've been in withdrawal for over a year!"

Not long after, Jim got an abscess from a dirty needle and almost lost his hand. He told me, "I have to quit. I have nothing left to lose!"

A few weeks later, in a drug stupor, he knocked over a candle and set his apartment on fire. After that, he was homeless. Again, he told me, "I have to quit. I have nothing left to lose!"

But he didn't or couldn't quit. One night a few months later, Jim died on a park bench in downtown Los Angeles. He had just turned 30 years old.

His was neither the first nor last drug-related funeral I attended, but it was for me one of the saddest. Here was a young man with so many gifts, but who was plagued by an addiction that seemingly nothing could overcome. He desperately desired to get clean. He came to meetings. He got a sponsor. He went to doctors and psychologists. But in the end, he succumbed to his addiction.

Faced with a case like Jim, a caring person asks, "Why?" Why did he die? Why was he unable to stop using drugs?

There is no satisfactory answer. Those of us in recovery often remind ourselves what we've been taught: addiction is a disease. The disease took him.

But what does it mean that addiction is a disease? Why is it that some who suffer find recovery, and so many others don't? Sometimes we think about it like cancer, from which some people recover and others don't.

What addiction is depends on who you ask. Google's dictionary, a reasonable indicator of the word's popular meaning, defines it as "the fact or condition of being addicted to a particular substance, thing, or activity." It lists as synonyms, "dependency, dependence, craving, habit, weakness, compulsion, fixation, [and] enslavement."[11] In popular usage, addiction covers a multitude of ills.

From a more scholarly perspective, the American Society of Addiction Medicine (ASAM) defines addiction this way:

> Addiction is a primary, chronic disease of brain reward, motivation, memory and related circuitry. Dysfunction in these circuits leads to characteristic biological, psychological, social and spiritual manifestations. This is reflected in an individual pathologically pursuing reward and/or relief by substance use and other behaviors.[12]

Addiction is, according to the ASAM, a *disease* located in the brain. But, as critics of the disease model rightly point out, if addiction is a disease, why isn't the *solution* for addiction medical? There are medical treatments for the withdrawal symptoms from drugs that are physically addictive, including alcohol. But the most widespread treatment for the *behavior* of addiction uses the Twelve Steps, originally stated by Alcoholics Anonymous in 1939. This "treatment" is not only non-medical, it's not even done by professionals! Twelve Step fellowships work on the principle of one sufferer helping another.

Clearly the disease model, as defined by the medical community, has shortcomings. One is that there is no standard definition of what a disease actually is.[13] Addiction

---

[11] "Addiction," Google (https://www.google.com/search?q=addiction+definition&oq=addiction+definition&aqs=chrome..69i57j0l5.9481j1j7&sourceid=chrome&ie=UTF-8, accessed July 26, 2019).

[12] "Definition of Addiction," ASAM.org, April 12, 2011 (https://www.asam.org/resources/definition-of-addiction, accessed July 26, 2019).

[13] Jackie Leach Scully, "What Is a Disease?" *EMBO Reports* Jul 2004, National Institute of Health (https://www.ncbi.nlm.nih.gov/pmc/articles/PMC1299105/, accessed March 27, 2019).

does have some characteristics of a disease, including physical dependence and biological changes to the body that differ from those who are not addicted.[14] Yet the category of disease does not fully describe the condition of addiction.

*   *   *   *

Psychologist Gerald May defines addiction as "any compulsive behavior that limits the freedom of human desire. It is caused by the attachment, or nailing, of desire to specific objects." May's definition is broad, and he lists among addictions not only drugs, alcohol, and gambling, but also children, dreams, fear of spiders, and ignorance. He also emphasizes that "*action* is essential to addiction."[15] For May, then, addiction is *behavioral*.

But if a person ceases to act on their compulsion for some period of time, is that person still an addict? Can an alcoholic, for example, after being sober for some time, return to social drinking? In most cases, the answer is an emphatic "No." The biological differences in the body of an alcoholic make it very unlikely for him or her to drink again in a controlled manner. And, without significant changes in *thinking*, behavioral changes alone are unlikely to keep a person sober for long. The behavioral model may help to explain some of the characteristics of chemical addiction, but it falls short of being a complete explanation.

Philosopher Kent Dunnington sees addiction as *habit* in its classical sense, as used by Aristotle, Augustine, and Thomas Aquinas.[16] For Dunnington, too, addiction is a set of

---

[14] James R. Milam and Katherine Ketcham, *Under the Influence: The Guide to the Myths and Realities of Alcoholism* (New York: Bantam Books, 1981), 35-36.

[15] Gerald G. May, *Addiction & Grace: Love and Spirituality in the Healing of Addictions* (New York: HarperCollins, 1988), 24-25, 38-39.

[16] Kent Dunnington, *Addiction and Virtue: Beyond the Models of Disease and Choice* (Downers Grove, IL: Intervarsity Press, 2011), 41.

behaviors that become entrenched through repetition. These entrenched behaviors, or habits, are acted upon without conscious thought. While Dunnington argues that voluntary choice cannot adequately describe addiction, he also challenges the disease model, suggesting instead that addiction is the result of entrenched, habitual behaviors.[17]

But how then do we explain the common observation that some addicts who have been in recovery in Twelve Step groups for multiple years, stop going to meetings and resume using drugs? Dunnington argues that the person "fail[ed] to develop genuine habits of sobriety."[18] There is no room in this model for regression. If, even after decades of sobriety, a person relapses, they never really changed in the first place.

This seems to defy reality. I have met people who seemed sincerely changed in their recovery. But after years or decades, they stopped doing those behaviors that maintained their recovery and relapsed into addiction. I don't find that the model of "habit" adequately explains addiction, either.[19]

On the other end of the spectrum, some Christian writers define addiction in biblical terms as "slavery to sin, drunkenness, idolatry, and spiritual strongholds."[20] For

---

[17] Ibid., 72.

[18] Ibid., 78.

[19] Dunnington describes addiction as a "false religion." This offers the possibility that the recovering addict finds an alternative "religion" that provides what is needed to live without drugs, but if or when he or she stops practicing that alternative religion, loses the benefit of it and becomes vulnerable to the old belief system again, with its attendant behaviors. Dunnington does not suggest this. I speculate that he may not consider this possibility because he may perhaps believe that the Twelve Steps do not qualify as a "true" religion because they do not center in Jesus Christ. I would also note here that, while I disagree with Dunnington on certain points, there is much in his analysis that is helpful in understanding addiction, and I am indebted to him for the analogy of addiction as "false worship."

[20] For example, Rick Nichols, *Dirty Discipleship: The Essential Nature of Recovery Ministry in Fulfilling the Great Commission* (Lynchburg, VA: Liberty University School of Divinity, 2017, unpublished doctoral thesis), 41.

them, addiction is an entirely spiritual failing. There is some truth to this, but it is often misinterpreted.

One problem often encountered with this approach is a problematic understanding of sin. Some view sin as action. Addicts, they say, *choose* to sin. They are sinful people, as differentiated from non-addicted believers who make better choices. But this is a defective understanding of sin. Sin, as properly understood in Christianity, is not action. Rather, sin is the *condition* of being broken, of being alienated from God. Dunnington writes, "[S]in is not something that we *do*, but something that we discover about who we *are*."[21]

A proper understanding of sin does help us understand addiction. Addicts are seeking to fill a perceived hole in themselves that is spiritual in nature. It's not unusual to hear someone in recovery explain, "I was trying to fill a God-shaped hole." We are estranged from God, which is the very definition of sin. To phrase this differently, we are separated from that which gives us meaning and makes us whole.

And yet the category of sin does not fully explain addiction, either. And it certainly doesn't appeal to the many addicts who are not Christian, and therefore has limited practical application. Approaching non-Christian people with the message, "You use drugs because you're a sinner," is unlikely to increase the recovery rate significantly.

Dunnington's phrasing that sin is "something we *discover* about who we are" is informative. The category of sin is something addicts may be able to hear once they are relieved of their immediate suffering, but it will only rarely get them off drugs to begin the recovery process.[22]

---

[21] Dunnington 132, emphasis in original.

[22] This is why the program Alcoholics Anonymous, which drew the Twelve Steps from a Christian discipleship program called the Oxford Groups, intentionally avoids talking about religion, insisting only that participants find "God as we [each individual] understood him." E.g. *Alcoholics Anonymous*, 59.

Which of these definitions is correct? Each offers something to the understanding of addiction, but none of them are sufficient by themselves. Addiction, and particularly substance addiction, is a complex phenomenon with characteristics of *all* these definitions, as well as other characteristics they don't consider. Each of these definitions describes one aspect of addiction. But none paint the full picture.

*   *   *   *

In some circles, it has become fashionable to avoid the terminology of addiction altogether in the interest of "harm reduction." Some, following the DSM-V, prefer the term "substance use disorder."[23] They argue that the terms "addict" and "addiction" are pejorative, opening the sufferer to stigmatization by society.

In my view, the answer to stigma with respect to drug addiction is not changing the terminology to pretend it doesn't exist, but education. Moreover, if we are not honest about the nature of addiction, as compared with risky use or dependence, we're enabling the sufferer's destruction.

A person addicted to a substance, who returns to it repeatedly even after separation, whose life is consumed by the quest for the substance, requires substantially different treatment than someone who does not exhibit these symptoms. Medical science has not yet been able to explain the phenomenon of addiction, but that does not make the distinction any less important. If anything, it suggests an even greater need for a comprehensive explanation.

---

[23] "DSM Criteria for Substance Abuse Disorders," *Primary Care Addiction Toolkit: Fundamentals of Addiction*, Portico (https://www.porticonetwork.ca/web/fundamentals-addiction-toolkit/introduction/dsm-critieria, accessed August 18, 2019).

The book *Alcoholics Anonymous* provides a somewhat more complex description of alcoholism, which can be expanded to include substance addiction in general: a physical allergy, a mental obsession, and a spiritual malady.

The chapter titled "The Doctor's Opinion" hypothesizes that the "phenomenon of craving," which causes an alcoholic person to crave alcohol once he or she takes a drink, is the manifestation of an "allergy." While the theory of allergy later proved to be inaccurate, the phenomenon of craving is real and caused the writers of the book to observe, "[T]here is no such thing as making a normal drinker out of an alcoholic." Once an alcoholic starts drinking, he or she develops an overpowering craving for more.[24]

This begs the question: Why does an alcoholic drink again after some period of not drinking? Here the mental obsession comes into play, the "utter inability to leave [alcohol] alone, no matter how great the necessity or wish." *Alcoholics Anonymous* describes several personal stories in which the alcoholic seems to have a desire to experience the pleasure formerly experienced at the early stages of drinking.[25] Alcoholics, and addicts in general, remain obsessed with re-experiencing the initial relief they found when they first started using their drug of choice, even long after the pleasure of using drugs has turned to misery.

Yet the book later develops a more satisfying answer for why alcoholics return to drinking: they have a "spiritual malady." This, the book claims, is the root of the problem. "When the spiritual malady is overcome, we straighten out mentally and physically."

This three-fold definition is one of the most comprehensive available. Yet it, too, has some shortcomings in terms of helping non-addicts to understand addiction and its symptoms. The following chapters will summarize and

---

[24] *Alcoholics Anonymous*, xxviii, 31.
[25] Ibid., 34-43.

explore the characteristics of addiction in order to provide a more complete picture that enables non-addicts to better understand and help those who struggle.

*   *   *   *

Before continuing, we should briefly consider what addiction is not. Addiction is not the same as dependence. More than 80 years ago, Alcoholics Anonymous distinguished between a "spree" drinker, a heavy drinker who may experience withdrawal symptoms, and an alcoholic.[26] The difference is simple: The "spree" drinker drinks too much when they drink, but they don't drink all the time. The heavy drinker may be physically dependent, and may go through withdrawal symptoms when they stop drinking. But they don't have the compulsion that causes them to return to drinking over and over again, as does the alcoholic.

For example, my friend Janice drank heavily after her husband died. She ended up in the hospital for alcohol poisoning. They dried her out and sent her to a Twelve Step program. But after a while, she realized that she had been drinking to manage her grief. She was not in danger of returning to alcohol. She stopped going to meetings, and hasn't had a drink in almost 20 years.

An alcoholic, in contrast, is obsessed with drinking again. The typical alcoholic reasoning might be more like this:

"I was only drinking to manage my grief. I'm not an alcoholic. Therefore, I can have one drink."

That first drink, of course, leads to the second, and the tenth, and the addiction to alcohol continues.

The same basic categories among drug addicts are now recognized by the scientific community. There are people who

---

[26] *Alcoholics Anonymous* 4th Edition, New York: Alcoholics Anonymous World Services, 2001, 20-21, 32.

abuse substances, engaging in high-risk behavior, who are not physically dependent on the substance. There are people who are dependent, but who are able to stay away from the drug once separated from it. And there are addicts, those perplexing people who return to using time after time.[27] The logical response to any problem with alcohol or drugs would be to avoid alcohol and drugs once the problem has been relieved. What makes an addict different is the insane decision to try it "just one more time."

Science has now confirmed what AA knew decades ago: there is a difference between dependence and addiction. One research hospital defines dependence as "when the body requires a specific dose of a particular drug, such as a prescription opioid, in order to prevent withdrawal symptoms." Addiction, on the other hand, includes "compulsive behaviors that manifest as cravings, an inability to control use, and continued use of the drug despite its harmful consequences."[28]

Any person who uses an addictive medication over a long period of time will become dependent. That is, they will experience withdrawal symptoms when they stop taking the medication. But only a small minority will become addicted, with the accompanying cravings and disregard for negative consequences.[29]

---

[27] DSM-IV recognized the former two categories as different, but DSM-V removed this distinction. Neither recognized the scientifically-verified distinction between dependence and addiction. All substance misuse is lumped into a spectrum called "Substance Use Disorder," which has no criteria to distinguish dependence from addiction. Marc Shuckit and Briget F. Grant, "DSM-5 Criteria for Substance Use Disorders: Recommendations and Rationale," *Am J Psychiatry* 2013; 170:834–851 (https://ajp.psychiatryonline.org/doi/pdf/10.1176/appi.ajp.2013.120607 82, accessed August 18, 2019).

[28] Justin Donofrio, "Opioids: Understanding Addiction Versus Dependence," HSS Hospital, May 2, 2018 (https://www.hss.edu/conditions_understanding-addiction-versus-dependence.asp, accessed August 7, 2019).

This book uses the term "addiction" to refer to the latter condition, in which the addict craves a substance and has no apparent control over his or her use of it.[30] It discusses that baffling condition, as distinct from other forms of substance abuse.[31]

---

[29] J. Chalmers Ballantine and Karl Steven Laforge, "Opioid dependence and addiction during opioid treatment of chronic pain," *Pain* 129(3):235–255, June 2007 DOI:10.1016/j.pain.2007.03.028.

[30] I consider alcoholism to be a specific type of addiction, and I include alcoholism in my examples because the symptoms are the same. The only difference is that alcohol is readily and legally available, while most other drugs people abuse are not.

[31] The DSM increasingly sees substance use as a spectrum, and there may be some wisdom to that perspective. However, addiction does have features and behaviors that are far less common in other degrees of substance use.

CHAPTER THREE
THE AUTHOR AS CASE STUDY

In the quest for a more complete explanation of addiction, I offer my own experience as an example. As a child, I had difficulty making friends and seemed to be the outcast at any gathering. I began using marijuana at age 15 because I wanted to be cool. We could describe this as peer pressure to conform, or modeling the behavior of others. But I think there's a better description: I began using drugs because I wanted to escape my loneliness. In a broader sense, I wanted to escape my world. As we will see later, this element of *escape* is essential to understanding how to recover from addiction.

What happened next was predictable: I quickly added other drugs to the menu, including stimulants and psychedelics. I liked the *effect* of drugs. They provided pleasure. There is, however, another way to look at this: they didn't actually cause me to be accepted into the social world, but they did stop the feelings of isolation. They were, in that sense, medication for a wound I had incurred. They were a *treatment* for trauma at a time in my life when no one, including myself, recognized that I even had trauma.

As I grew older and eventually reached the legal drinking age, alcohol became more available. Unlike others drugs, I didn't start using alcohol gradually. The very first time I drank, at age 16, I drank to excess. Afterward, I drank at every possible opportunity. This is where the physical disease aspect of addiction is most evident. Scientists tell us that the body of an alcoholic, for example, actually processes alcohol differently than that of a non-alcoholic, converting the alcohol into substances that trigger an overpowering physical craving for more. This can be caused by drinking, or it can be passed down genetically.[32] While my parents are not alcoholic, there are plenty of alcoholics in my family tree.

When a person finds relief in substances, seeking and using substances becomes a way of life. I was gainfully employed most of the time for one simple reason: I needed money to buy drugs and alcohol. The quest to earn money, find drugs, and get high became my normal routine. It became a *habit*, in the classical sense expressed by Aristotle and Augustine: I was habituated to live for the purpose of getting high. My thoughts and actions became accustomed to living that way. Drugs provided a framework for daily living. Over time, any other way of life began to seem impossible.

At the same time, drugs became the purpose for my existence. I suffered from the wounds of my earlier traumas. The world seemed too painful to live in without chemical pain relief. Drugs and alcohol were the only things that made me feel better. The goals commonly expressed in the world, such as saving money, buying a house, and getting a more expensive car, seemed to have no relevance for me. Drugs made me feel better. My car didn't. Eventually, getting and using drugs became the sole purpose for my life—my *telos*, my ultimate goal.

During one period of unemployment when I was 19, my money ran low. For weeks, I ate rice and Jello in order to save my money for alcohol and drugs. This is not a normal choice. Decisions like these make the addict different from other people in purpose as well as behavior. This is especially true in a society in which drugs are criminalized. Addicts constantly face ostracism, financial ruin through job loss, and even incarceration because of our addiction.

---

[32] See for example Milam and Ketcham, 35-36.

I remember thinking not that what I *did* was illegal, but that I *was* illegal because of my addiction. I felt like, and indeed was, an outcast from society trying to pretend I belonged. The secrecy involved separates us from family, coworkers, and friends. I recall sitting in an office with two other men, listening them to describe the family events they had engaged in over the weekend. I could not join the conversation because all I'd done was drink and use drugs. My addiction began to define who I was. It became my *identity*.

As I pursued my addiction, I took actions that most people would consider immoral. I lied. I drove under the influence. I sold drugs in order to use the profit for my own supply. Sometimes I stole. My moral code was at least different than that of society.

Some would have considered me immoral. But Kent Dunnington makes a startling claim: Addiction "is in fact a deeply moral undertaking directed toward the attainment of particular moral and intellectual goods."[33] In other words, addicts *are* moral, but the object of their morality is not society, not the economy, and not God. Rather, our morality consists of devotion to the substance that gives us relief. We are deeply committed. But that commitment causes actions that deviate from societal norms.

*   *   *   *

The last few years of my addiction were miserable. The drugs no longer gave me the relief I sought. I tried different substances and different combinations. I used more, overdosing several times. I took more risks getting them, and used substances that had obvious and unknown impurities. I didn't care if I died. I believed that death would be preferable

---

[33] Dunnington, 83.

to the life I was living. Many times I woke in the morning wondering, "Why am I still alive? Why can't I just die?" I had become actively self-destructive.

The obvious question here is why, if I hated my life of addiction, I didn't just stop. This brings us to the crux of the problem, which is rarely clear at the beginning of the process. I *did* try to stop, many times. Once I went a whole week without drinking or using. But I felt empty inside. I had no purpose. Something was missing. There was a hole in me that nothing else filled. I was also angry all the time.

One day, toward the end of that week, one of my coworkers told me, "Whatever you're doing, it isn't working. I hope you'll go back to doing what you were doing before."

I didn't need to be told twice, and got high again that very night.

This highlights the two final characteristics I will consider. First, I used because I had a deep longing for something I didn't find in the world. I would later learn it was a spiritual longing. This is something our society doesn't offer answers for. We are given freedom to determine our own spiritual path, if any. Most people seem content to focus on economic status and their families. Others go to church on Sunday. There are few options for those who experience a deep spiritual longing that needs to be filled daily.

Because of this, I also experienced deep despair. My life of addiction no longer worked. Neither did the ways of the world. I couldn't see another option, except death. Many addicts begin their drug use because of feelings of despair and disillusionment with the world around them. As their addiction turns to misery, they despair of life with or without drugs. When I was using, I used to say, "There's no such thing as an accidental overdose." That is obviously a generalization. But many people in advanced addiction no longer care whether they live or die.

I use my own story to illustrate the typical characteristics of substance addiction, which include:

- Desire to escape (disillusionment with the world)
- Initial pleasure (choice)
- Dull feelings of pain (trauma treatment)
- Disease (physical compulsion and/or dependence)
- Habituation (way of life, psychological compulsion)
- Purpose for living (provides meaning)
- Separation from the norm (threat of incarceration, outcast/judged by society)
- Identity (definition of self)
- Moral framework (how to live)
- Spiritual longing
- Self-destructive behavior (self-harm and even death)
- Despair (loss of hope)

If we are to understand addiction, we must understand these complex features. The next chapters will explore each of them in more detail.

D. J. Mitchell

CHAPTER FOUR
THE TRAUMA CONNECTION

As I found drugs that eased my pain, I encouraged my friends to try them. As my choice of drugs advanced, so did the resulting consequences. Several people's lives were destroyed after I convinced them to try certain drugs.

When I got clean and sober, one of the instructions I received was to make amends for the things I had done. This "evangelism" was high on my list. Now in recovery, I felt I had committed a wrong I could never set right.

My wise sponsor told me two things. First, I *had* committed a wrong that I could not fully set right. My amends were to spend my life ready to help anyone who sought rescue from addiction. That is a promise I have kept.

His second piece of wisdom was this: "People who are not addicts don't stick needles in their arms."

Herein lies one of the problems with the disease model: We know that the disease aspect of addiction causes a person to crave more once they have begun drinking or using. *But what causes them to begin drinking or using in the first place?* Alcoholism may perhaps be explained because light or moderate drinking is socially acceptable. But, as a wise woman in recovery once told me, "There's no such thing as social heroin use."

This chapter will attempt to answer this question: Why do those who become addicts begin using at all?

When I was four years old, an older cousin came to stay with us. He was probably only six, though to me he seemed almost an adult. He shared my room, and was supposed to play with me. But he played rough. He would hit me, and knock me off the bed. I threatened to tell my mom, but he said, "She won't believe you." Eventually, I did tell my mom. She asked him if it was true, and of course he denied it. So my mom didn't believe me. Instead of getting rescued, I was punished for lying.

This became one of the formative experiences of my childhood. I learned that people can't be trusted, the world isn't fair, there is no justice, and there was nothing I could do about it. My subsequent experiences seemed to confirm these "facts," perhaps because that's what I expected to happen. When you're looking for disappointment, that's the part of life you see.

This experience taught me not to trust society. Its goals, its morals, and its structures were, in my mind, hypocritical and empty. By the time I was fifteen, I'd had enough of the world. I began to contemplate suicide.

Instead, I started using drugs.

My experience is far from unique. One of the Twelve Steps is to take a "moral inventory" and share it with someone. Over the years, I've heard a lot of inventories, and many of them include childhood abuse or trauma.

When I met Derrick, he was struggling with methamphetamine addiction. I learned that Derrick's father had left when Derrick was young, and his mother had moved in with her sister. The sister's husband, Derrick's uncle, used to beat him for no apparent reason.

After being convicted on drug charges, Tim chose diversion to a drug treatment center rather than going to prison. In his inventory, Tim reported that his mom had remarried when he was ten, and Tim's older step-sisters had sexually abused him.

Jack, who was serving a 20-year prison sentence for robbery because he needed money for drugs, had been beaten regularly by his father.

I've heard dozens of similar stories. Yet it's difficult to tell if trauma is a universal characteristic of addiction. Often, the incident is just accepted as part of life, and given no particular attention. The life of an addict is far from normal. We face daily struggles, withdrawal symptoms, violence, fear because of the circles in which we travel, and incarceration is common. In that reality, it's easy to accept an early childhood experience as just "more of the same," background noise, when in fact it may be a precursor to what followed.

Sometimes the incident isn't even remembered until the addicted person gets clean and begins to do some significant healing work with therapists or spiritual healers. I've known both men and women who didn't realize they'd been physically or sexually abused until well into their recovery.

For example, Lorraine was a friend I met in meetings who was recovering from alcoholism. Like many addicts, she had a history of sexual promiscuity that included several abusive relationships. She'd been sober more than ten years when she remembered that her father had sexually abused her.

Susan, another recovering alcoholic, was 37 years old when she began to have memories of being sexually abused. At first she thought she was going crazy. But as the memories became clearer, she realized that the abuser was her favorite uncle, who had died a few years before. This was later confirmed. The man had confessed on his deathbed that he had abused several of his nieces.

*　　　　*　　　　*　　　　*

The role of trauma in addiction cannot be overstated. Trauma specialist Carolyn Yoder describes trauma as,

[O]verwhelm[ing] our usual ability to cope with and respond to threat. It often results in long-term, debilitating, cyclical symptoms. These may include hyper-arousal, anger, depression, apathy, inability to trust, or find meaning in life, acting in and acting out, and difficulty in relationships and communication. It causes the victim of trauma to feel powerless.[34]

In other words, the experience of powerlessness at the time of the traumatic event continues to resurface in other situations and relationships long after the event itself, causing our minds to see threats where they don't exist.

This powerlessness in the face of the traumatic event is a key component. Trauma researcher Bessel A. van der Kolk reports that if a person can maintain some sense of control over the situation, "however small," they are less likely to develop PTSD. "Only when they are faced with inevitable catastrophe do the victims experience intense feelings of loss and desertion... once a person dissociates, he becomes incapable of goal-directed action."[35]

Trauma shatters our world. It violates trust and causes us to withdraw from society. John Swinton, a theologian and mental health worker, notes that trauma even causes us to question God. We cannot answer the underlying question, "Why?" What kind of God allows bad things to happen to good people—and even to innocent children?[36]

---

[34] Carolyn Yoder, *The Little Book of Trauma Healing: When Violence Strikes and Community is Threatened* (New York: Good Books, 2005), 15, 18, 33.

[35] Bessel A. van der Kolk, "Coping," *In Terror's Grip: Healing the Ravages of Trauma* (http://www.traumacenter.org/products/pdf_files/terrors_grip.pdf, accessed August 6, 2019).

[36] John Swinton, *Raging with Compassion: Pastoral Responses to the Prblem of Evil* (Grand Rapids, MI: Wm. B. Eerdmans Publishing, 2007), 9,

The effects of trauma continue long after the incident occurs. Van der Kolk writes,

> Traumatized people rarely realize that their intense feelings and reactions are based on past experience. They blame their present surroundings for the way they feel and thereby rationalize their feelings. The almost infinite capacity to rationalize in this way keeps them from having to confront the helplessness and horror of their past..."[37]

Maria had five years in recovery when I met her in a Twelve Step meeting. She was an angry woman, and she scared me a little. But at the time, I too was struggling with anger, so I talked to her about her experience, hoping to learn how to manage my own anger. Maria explained that she had begun to recognize that when she got angry, she wasn't really angry at the person in front of her—she was angry at someone who had abused her in the distant past.

Imagine this pattern as an ongoing coping mechanism in a person who has not begun to heal from their trauma. You say something to me. It triggers an old wound, and I feel hurt, scared, and powerless. I don't blame the cousin who abused me. I don't blame my mother for not believing me. I blame you, the person in front of me. In my mind, *you* hurt me, even though it's clearly not your fault. I leave the encounter hurting, and believing that the world is full of people who have it in for me.

For an addict, the only possible response is to return to the substance that has never failed me. I drink or use drugs.

For someone who is not yet an addict, drugs start to sound like a good idea.

92.
[37] Van der Kolk, "Reliving, Not Remembering."

Trauma also causes depression, and depression is statistically linked to addiction. Adolescents aged 12-17 who have experienced a major depressive episode (MDE) are twice as likely to drink alcohol and three times as likely to have a substance use disorder as their peers who did not have an MDE.[38]

In short, a person who has experienced trauma is predisposed to anger and depression, may fail to find meaning or purpose in life, cannot trust God, and, in a hyper-aroused state, expects the worst to happen. Their ongoing feelings of pain they blame on present circumstances, putting them at odds with their family, their friends, and society as a whole. This is a person in pain, who may not even be aware of the source of their pain. They may have been hurting for so long that they don't even realize they are in pain, they just feel like they have always felt.

This is a person predisposed to addiction.

The high incidence of childhood trauma has only recently been recognized. The American Psychological Association (APA) describes the field as "relatively young." Recent estimates of the number of children who experience sexual abuse range from 25% to 43%. While the report notes variation in the survey results, the *low* estimate is that one in four American children is sexually abused.[39] A 2013 report indicates that 41% of children aged 0-17 surveyed reported having been physically assaulted *in the past year*. The ages in which the highest incidence of assaults occurred were 2-5

---

[38] Bose, "Co-Occurring Substance Use and Mental Health Issues" (https://www.samhsa.gov/data/sites/default/files/cbhsq-reports/NSDUHFFR2017/NSDUHFFR2017.htm#mde1, accessed August 6, 2019).

[39] "Children and Trauma: Update for Mental Health Professionals," 2008 Presidential Task Force on Posttraumatic Stress Disorder and Trauma in Children and Adolescents (https://www.apa.org/pi/families/resources/children-trauma-update, accessed August 6, 2019).

and 10-13.[40] The government agency SAMHSA reports that one in five high school students has experienced bullying.[41]

Not all of these victims develop the long-term effects of trauma. APA states, "Although most return to baseline functioning, a substantial minority of children develop severe acute or ongoing psychological symptoms (including PTSD symptoms)..." Yet there are insufficient resources for diagnosis and healing of trauma in children. The APA continues, "Most children and adolescents with traumatic exposure or trauma-related psychological symptoms are not identified and consequently do not receive any help. Even those who are identified as in need of help frequently do not obtain any services."[42]

In the absence of healing, this "significant minority" of children who need help becomes a pool of potential future addicts. In fact, SAMHSA lists drug and alcohol abuse as one of four indicators, along with depression, eating disorders, and risky sexual behavior, of unhealed trauma in middle and high school students.[43]

Referring to the list of addiction characteristics in the previous chapter, past trauma creates in the sufferer a desire to *escape* this world, the attraction of relief from their feelings (*pleasure*), and the need for *treatment*, even if self-administered. Untreated trauma is a common precursor to addiction.

I cannot make the blanket statement that all addicts suffer from childhood trauma. There are surely other causes. But the high incidence of trauma as a factor in addiction

---

[40] David Finkelhor, *et al*, "Violence Crime, and Abuse Exposure in a National Sample of Children and Youth," *JAMA Pediatrics* May 13 2013 (http://www.unh.edu/ccrc/pdf/05-13%20PED%20childhood%20exposure%20to%20violence.pdf, accessed August 6, 2019).

[41] "Understanding Child Trauma," Substance Abuse and Mental Health Services Administration (https://www.samhsa.gov/child-trauma/understanding-child-trauma, accessed August 6, 2019).

[42] Ibid.

[43] Ibid.

cannot be overlooked. It is one of the primary reasons people begin drinking and using.

The problem, of course, is that healing from trauma is a complex process that requires the sufferer to be present and self-aware. Once substance abuse begins, active addiction works against those requirements. Typically, a person cannot even begin to heal their past hurts until they gain stable recovery.

Healing is difficult and emotionally-challenging work. An easier path is for the addict to return to the old ways of coping. Thus, while trauma is an important precursor to addiction, healing trauma is not the first step in recovery. There is a great deal of foundational work that must be done first.

CHAPTER FIVE
ADDICTION: A WAY OF LIFE

Oscar, a man in his thirties, had been in jail for two years. During that time, he came in contact with the pastor of a local church. He made a decision to change his life. When Oscar was released, he came out with high hopes for change. He began attending church weekly. He found a place to stay in a small apartment next to the home of a congregant, and got a job. With this income, he was able to rent an apartment of his own. He was even working to reconcile with his children.

The church leadership began to plan a system of accountability for Oscar so he would have someone to be responsible to in his new life. But all was not well. The congregation, with the best of intentions, expected that Oscar would rejoin the "real world." He had a job and a place to stay. That should be enough, right?

It wasn't. One problem was that the church operated on a system of monthly leadership meetings. It took six months to create a plan.

For another, despite their good intentions, those involved failed to grasp that the central truth for addicts is that the world has failed them. A plan to simply return an addict to the world doesn't work.

The same week the church became ready to implement its plan, Oscar disappeared. He surfaced months later, incarcerated once more for drug-related offenses.

You see, as a drug user or a drinker passes into the realm of addiction, his or her perspective on life changes. The substance provides a necessary benefit. As described in the previous chapter, it allows escape from a world that is unendurable. And although the pleasure will eventually fade and be replaced with misery, it still dulls the underlying pain with which the addict starts using—pain that is only magnified as the addiction progresses with its accompanying shame, disillusionment, and hardships. Although the substance is the cause of these increasing woes, it is also the only solution the addict knows. And, as is typical with trauma survivors, the addict does not blame the drug, but the people and situations he or she currently faces.

The substance becomes the addict's only respite, the central focus of life. It is what makes life worth living, to the extent that life remains worth living.

We may start using drugs because we believe they will help us to continue working. But after a while, we work in order to continue using drugs. Faced with the choice of giving up drugs or giving up the job, to an addict the answer is obvious. Drug use must continue. In the choice between drugs and family, the answer is the same.

Addiction thus becomes a way of life. Our waking hours are spent thinking about, seeking, planning for, and using whatever substance it is that we are addicted to. The drug becomes our *purpose* for life. Every action and every decision supports our drug use. It is the one thing that matters above all else.

Oscar, much as he wanted to change his life, was faced with a terrifying prospect: He didn't know what to do with his time each day. The hours once spent at home feeding his addiction were now empty, idle, and meaningless.

This is something we usually can't admit to others. The people around us seem happy with work, sleep, and television. We're not. We may not recognize all this, but we feel like there's something wrong with us. We're different.

Why are we different? Because we're addicts. And without some hope and guidance, no matter how much willpower we have, we will eventually return to the only way of life that has ever "filled" us.

Because the drug has become the focus of life, at some point in our addiction, the drug also sets the *moral framework* that guides our actions. In my own case, I said I would never steal. For years, I kept that code. I lied, I sold drugs, and I pretended to run out when one of my friends had some. But I didn't steal.

One night, I was desperate. I needed drugs badly. I went to a supplier's house to buy some. While he was in the back room measuring out what I wanted, he left his own personal supply sitting on the table.

I took half of it.

I later stole from the company that employed me. I stole food from the local market. I stole alcohol from people when no one was looking. I had become a thief. Despite my moral intentions, when faced with a choice between the morals I'd been taught and the pursuit of my addiction, the addiction came first.

I'm not alone in abandoning the moral code I was taught. I've known both men and women who prostituted themselves for drug money. Kendall installed alarm systems on veterinary hospitals, then later went back and used the codes to steal drugs. Dean would stand beside a car outside the mall, telling people he was out of gas and asking them for five dollars. It wasn't his car. He didn't even own a car!

I met Jennifer before I got clean and sober. She had three children, and a neck injury had left her unable to work. She received disability. She paid her rent, but the rest of the money she spent on drugs and alcohol. Her kids wore worn-out clothes and panhandled for food money.

Even then, those choices disgusted me. But I was in no position to judge her. Despite my discomfort with her decisions, my friends and I still came by to drink her alcohol and share her drugs.

These are morally abhorrent actions. They lead some people to conclude that addicts are immoral. But for an addict, the morals of society no longer apply. In our minds, and also in a broader sense, society has failed us. Kent Dunnington argues that addiction is in fact deeply moral.[44] Our moral code is just different. It seeks to support the central truth of our lives: we need our drug of choice to live.

This "truth" is, of course, false. But until we find an alternative, we believe it to be true. I recall, in my early attempts at recovery, sitting alone at home trying to convince myself that I didn't have to use. People had told me. I wanted to believe them. But that contradicted my very real experience. Alone, I had no hope of staying clean. Sooner or later, I would give in to that old belief—because I had no real belief that anything else was possible. And for months, I did give in: after a week, or a few days, or one day. The possibility of change was not yet fully real to me.

*   *   *   *

At some point, our addiction becomes our *identity*. It defines our understanding of ourselves. Part of this is the redefinition of our lives and morals to support our addiction. It's what our lives revolve around. Part of it is the response of society to addiction, and the necessary secrecy we live with. Even alcoholics, despite alcohol being legal, have to hide the frequency and amount of their drinking to avoid judgment from the people around them.

---

[44] Dunnington, 83.

How does a person identify themselves? Who we are includes both what group we belong to and what makes us different. We choose both elements of inclusion and exclusion. For example, I'm an American, like almost everyone around me. When I travel to other countries, that makes me different. I am white, like most of the people around me. I am Christian, which distinguishes me from some other people. I am *not* a Republican or a Democrat. I claim independence from the two parties most people identify with. Even though I currently live in the South, I still identify as a Red Sox fan, a statement that I'm not from here.

For a practicing addict, the differences between the self and other "normal" people grows larger over time. The addict is not, in any conventionally recognized way, normal. Our narrow interests are not normal, nor is our behavior. I couldn't join in the conversation with my coworkers about what I'd done over the weekend, for example, because I couldn't *admit* what I'd done over the weekend. The difference between my life and "normal" could not be ignored. My choice was either to be silent, or to lie. Sometimes, during a break, I would sneak off to contact a drug supplier to make arrangements for after work, a call I couldn't afford to let anyone else overhear. This kind of situation begins to define our identity by the difference, even if that identity is unspoken.

One day, while I was a practicing addict, someone knocked on the door of my apartment while my friends and I were getting high. We put everything into a cigar box on the table, and I opened the door.

In walked my landlady's husband, an elderly man who was very drunk. He sat down at the table without an invitation and joined our conversation. At one point, out of curiosity, he reached for the cigar box that contained our drugs and paraphernalia. I immediately stopped him. Being drunk is one thing. Being an addict carries an entirely different status in our society.

If you had asked me about my identity at that moment, I would have admitted I was an addict—but (I would have claimed) I was *certainly* not a drunk. There was almost a sense of pride in being different. I might have even used Christian-sounding language: "I am not of this world." I was different. I had rejected the American Dream. I'd recognized that what I saw was a lie: that the "dream" could never fill the hole in me.[45]

At other times, my identity as an addict came with a sense of shame and fatalism. I never had any money because I spent it all on drugs and alcohol. I dreamed of going on adventures, but rarely left the house. I once had a chance to see the Rolling Stones in concert, but passed it up because I needed the money to get high. I often regretted that choice later in life.

I recall a supervisor's judgmental look when my car broke down and I rode the bus to work for several weeks. He said, "I know what you make, and I know where you live. Why don't you have money to fix your car?"

I couldn't answer, because the answer was unacceptable: I spent all my money on drugs.

*　　　　*　　　　*　　　　*

Even though I sometimes wanted to quit drinking and using, I didn't believe I could. I couldn't imagine any other way of living. More than that, in my deepest self-understanding, I

---

[45] Dunnington (107-109) argues that the rise in addiction corresponds to an increasing recognition that the American Dream (or, as he puts it, consumerism) is merely a distraction from the failure of society to guide us in finding what is truly important in life. He is not the first to argue the spiritually unsatisfying nature of consumerism, but he may be the first to link it to the rise on addiction.

wasn't just addicted, I *was* an addict. This is what addicts do. I had no choice.

This intersection of addiction as a way of life, a moral code, and an identity suggests another category that can be helpful for understanding it: Addiction can be compared to religion.[46]

Pioneering sociologist Emile Dirkheim defined religion as, "a unified system of beliefs and practices relative to sacred things, that is to say, things set apart and forbidden -- beliefs and practices which unite into one single moral community called a Church, all those who adhere to them."[47]

We can see these elements present in addiction: a system of beliefs and practices that center around that which is set apart as ultimately significant—the substance—from which derives a moral code. While it would be stretching credibility to describe the subculture of addiction as a "church," it is certainly a community set apart from society by its beliefs, practices, and divergent moral code.[48] Like religion, addiction seeks to identify the meaning of life—something that modern secular society fails to define for us.[49]

---

[46] This develops a theme proposed by Dunnington (142-145), and I am deeply indebted to him for this insight.

[47] Emile Durkheim, *The Elementary Forms of the Religious Life* (1912), cited in Robert Alun Jones, *Emile Durkheim: An Introduction to Four Major Works* (Beverly Hills, CA: Sage Publications, Inc., 1986, http://durkheim.uchicago.edu/Summaries/forms.html, accessed August 17, 2019), 115-155.

[48] It is unpopular in our culture to allow religion to have moral beliefs that diverge from the societal norm, though in fact the fundamental teachings of most religions do, whether or not this is evident in practice. Perhaps the most famous popular example is Con-Agra's campaign for Hebrew National kosher franks, which claimed, "We answer to a higher authority" than the federal government. Stuart Elliot, "Humor and 'a higher authority' help spice up a new campaign for Hebrew National franks," *Times* (New York), May 23 1997 (https://www.nytimes.com/1997/05/23/business/humor-higher-authority-help-spice-up-new-campaign-for-hebrew-national-franks.html, accessed August 17, 2019).

[49] Ron Givens, "Chapter 15: Religion," William Little, ed., *Introduction to Sociology*, 1st Canadian Edition (https://opentextbc.ca/introductiontosociology/chapter/chapter-15-

Religion offers a way of life, a moral code, and an identity. It provides a purpose and reason for living. At its best, it motivates people to live better lives, work for positive change, challenge injustice in the world, and even risk their lives for others. Some would say that a true religion *should* resemble addiction.[50] Like addiction, true religion should place its own values above those of the world, regardless of the cost. Of course, false religions may promote violence and self-destruction instead. In this sense, addiction plays the role of a false religion, a belief system that motivates unhealthy behaviors, regardless of the cost.

Reform theologian Martin Luther wrote, "Whatever your heart clings to and confides in, that is really your God."[51] For addicts, that "whatever" is our drug of choice.

Addicts practice "religion" with the intensity of a monastic order. Like monks who recite the psalms seven times each day and reflect upon God in their work, addicts "worship" their drug daily, and think about it constantly even when they are not actually using it.

An understanding of addiction cannot ignore the practical implications of this "religious" devotion. Oscar, the man who sought help in church, had a good-paying job, a place to stay, and a congregation that cared about him. But, as a person who had given up drugs, he had lost a familiar way of life, his moral compass, and even his sense of self. He needed a new daily discipleship to replace the one he had given up. Without it, returning to his former way of life was virtually inevitable.

For most people, their lives and identities are related to their daily activities: family, job, hobbies, and sports teams.

religion/, accessed August 17, 2019).
[50] See, for example, Dunnington, 169.
[51] Martin Luther, *Luther's Large Catechism,* trans. John Nicholas Lenker (Minneapolis: Luther, 1908), 44, cited in James K. A. Smith, *You Are What You Love: The Spiritual Power of Habit* (Grand Rapids, MI: Brazos Press, 2016), 23.

For an addict, meaning and identity come from the pursuit of drugs.

An addict who stops using loses the daily activity and structure that formerly gave life meaning. There is a hole in their self-understanding begging to be filled, and it can't be filled by the kind of life that didn't work for them before they became addicted. If we expect an addict to return to the ways of the world, the ways of "normal" society, *our basic assumption about how an addict stops using is fatally flawed.*

CHAPTER SIX
OUR INNER LIFE

I was about five years clean and sober when I was first diagnosed with depression. A therapist referred me to a psychiatrist, who prescribed antidepressants. This turned out not to be a good idea for me—I reacted badly to them. But in the third week of taking them, there was a brief period in which I suddenly felt better than I had ever felt before. I was *happy*! I had never known what that felt like. Street drugs had made me feel better than I'd felt without them, but they had never made feel happy.

Up to that point, I didn't know I was depressed because it's how I'd always felt. I had nothing to compare it to. I'd never felt *not* depressed. How can you know what normal feelings are if you've never felt them?

Most addicts come to our addiction as wounded people. We have experienced trauma, abuse, and abandonment. We may not be aware of the magnitude of our own pain. We can't remember *not* being in pain. Pain is our normal state.

Drugs relieve that pain. That relief is temporary but effective, at least in the short term. It plays the role of treatment for a problem the addict doesn't understand. It is the only relief we have ever known.

But drugs don't heal the pain. And drugs don't fill the emptiness an addict feels, they only make it easier to ignore. They are the best treatment the addict has yet found, but there remains a deep, hidden longing for true healing, for an end to the emptiness of our existence.

That emptiness is one of the mysteries of addiction. Singer-songwriter Peter Case describes it as, "There's a hole in your soul where the wind blows through."[52] We feel like there's something missing, something we imagine that "normal" people were born with and we weren't.

Alcoholics Anonymous refers to this as a "spiritual malady." While it never defines this precisely, it does give hints about the nature of this malady. We "chose to believe that our human intelligence was the last word..." We were "confused and baffled by the seeming futility of existence..."[53] In other words, we had nothing beyond ourselves to look to, and that did not give life any satisfactory meaning.

This is not a medical problem. The meaning of life is the realm of philosophers and theologians. It goes to the root of our worldview and affects our entire outlook on life. After all, if life has no purpose, why *not* pursue drugs even in the face of likely self destruction? What does it matter?

Alcoholics Anonymous makes a somewhat startling claim: we don't need to be a philosopher or theologian to fill this basic human need for purpose. What we need is some concept of "a power greater than ourselves," which for most westerners means some conception of God.[54]

This, then, is the nature of the spiritual malady: we have a deep spiritual longing for that which is Ultimate.

For those who come from a theistic background such as Christianity or Judaism, this presents less of a problem. We already have a concept of God. We may not, and probably do not, have a relationship with God. We may even be angry at God for the wounds we carry and the perception that life has been unfair to us, whether or not we're aware of the specific nature of our wounds. But the concept is not foreign to us.

---

[52] Peter Case, "Travellin' Light," *The Man With the Blue Post-Modern Fragmented Neo-Traditionalist Guitar* (Geffen Records, 1989).
[53] *Alcoholics Anonymous*, 64, 49-51.
[54] Ibid., 50.

For those who come from backgrounds that do not believe in God, such as Buddhism or atheism, this can be more challenging. Yet there are thousands of people from such backgrounds in recovery in Twelve Step programs. Some see the group itself as their higher power; others put their faith in the process of the Twelve Steps.

Doug was one such person. I met him in a Twelve Step meeting, and he was a militant atheist. One might even call him an evangelist. He didn't believe in God, and he would try to convince others that they shouldn't either.

For Doug, his higher power was the belief that society could be changed for the better. Although he was white, he'd grown up in a minority neighborhood in a major city, and he related to the problems of the urban poor. He'd been beaten by police in a protest march many years before, and had a huge scar in his face and spoke with an impediment as a result. In his addiction, these physical wounds had fueled his resentment at the world. In recovery, they motivated him to live a simple life and work for the benefit of those who were disadvantaged.

One day, a few years into my friendship with Doug, I got a strange phone call from him. In it, he said words I never expected to hear.

"I found God," he told me.

At the time I was still struggling with my own belief, and Doug proceeded to try to convince me to believe in God with the same fervor he formerly used in his atheism.

The point is, many who come into recovery as atheists or other types of nonbelievers eventually do come to believe in some conception of God. Having worked the Steps as an agnostic myself, I can attest that believing in God is not required. But I can also tell you that for me, finding a purpose for life *without* believing in God was not easy.

Now that I have become Christian, I can also attest that there really is a God who works in our lives, and that is a great comfort to me. But the purpose of relating this is not to convince you of the correctness of my personal religious views. It is, rather, to emphasize that such views can play an important role in recovery. This book is about addiction, not religion.

*   *   *   *

Addicts have a deep spiritual longing that they may not even be aware of. They desperately seek a connection with some thing or purpose greater than themselves. They haven't found this connection in the world or its churches. The only reliable connection they have found is with their drug of choice.

Ironically, the drug does give them a purpose. The pursuit of the drug becomes their reason for living. This they do without regard to negative consequences. If life has no meaning other than to avoid the pain, of what value is tomorrow?

Billy was an addict who had been coming to meetings for a couple of years. He'd stay clean for a few weeks, then use again. One day, I heard that Billy was in the hospital after an overdose of Oxycontin, a prescription opioid he'd bought on the street. Billy was in a coma, and was not expected to wake up.

Billy's family gathered around him and prayed. Then they had the doctor disconnect Billy's life support. To the shock of everyone present, he woke up!

But his body was badly damaged. His kidneys had failed, and he had severe nerve damage. Doctors told Billy he'd be on dialysis the rest of his life, and he would never walk again.

Three weeks later, Billy's kidneys began working, once again defying medical predictions. He healed enough to go home, but walked with crutches. Over time, he gave up the crutches for a cane, and then was able to walk without a cane, and eventually without a brace. Today, he walks without any sign of the damage he inflicted on himself.

I relate this story because this was not the last time Billy used. A few months after leaving the hospital, he again used Oxycontin—the same drug that had almost killed him. Without a purpose for life other than the drugs, Billy didn't really care if he lived or died. What may seem like an insane decision was perfectly logical given his underlying belief: life was not worth living for its own sake.

After this last relapse, Billy began working the Steps in earnest. He did recover, overcame his spiritual malady, went to college, and now works in law enforcement. This man, who formerly didn't care if he lived or died, found a purpose for life. Without such a purpose, life has no value and is easily a second choice to drugs.

This is true regardless of how miserable our addiction makes us. The last three years of my using were awful. I could rarely afford enough drugs to quell the cravings I had. The lies, the stealing, and the embarrassing things I did while high or drunk, weighed on me. This was not the person I wanted to be. Many mornings, I woke up and asked, "Why can't I just die?" But despite the misery, I kept using because I couldn't imagine any other way of living.

Our spiritual life plays another role that is just as important. Most often, addicts are presented with two choices: continue our addiction, or return to the "real" world of jobs, homes, and families. We've tried that "real" world, and found that it doesn't fill the hole in us. Over time, no matter how bad our addiction gets and how miserable it makes us, we lose hope that we can live any other way. We *believe* that addiction is our only option. Only the drug can fill those empty places in us.

Alice was a heroin addict who turned to prostitution for drug money. When I met her, she was desperate to get off heroin. Her life was a mess. She had lost her children, and she hated what she had to do to support her habit. But she wasn't interested in a drug rehabilitation program. She didn't believe she could get off drugs. Instead, she planned to switch from heroin to cocaine. I lost track of her after that, and have no idea how her life turned out.

Fred was a traveling salesman, an older man who was passing through town. He was also an alcoholic, and in physically bad shape. He called the local Twelve Step office for help, and they asked me to go visit him.

Fred really wanted to quit. He was diabetic.

"The doctor told me that if I don't stop drinking, I'm going to lose my feet," he confessed. "I have to stop."

He went to some meetings with me, but told me very frankly that he was afraid of the withdrawal symptoms if he stopped drinking. He said he needed an inpatient program. I found one that could take him in two days, and he agreed to go.

On the day Fred was supposed to go to the hospital, I knocked on the door of his cheap motel room.

"I can't go," he told me. "Nolan Ryan is pitching tonight, and he's my hero."

No amount of logic could convince him that going to the hospital was more important than watching a baseball game on TV, even at the cost of his feet. This is not a logical decision. And it almost certainly wasn't the truth. More likely, he had no hope whatever that he could actually stop drinking and live a sober life.

This *hopelessness*, this despair, makes recovery impossible. If our only choices are addiction or a return to the world that fails to give us meaning, then there is no hope for us. If we don't *believe* there is another way of life, we will always return to the one that has sustained us, no matter how miserable it may be.

Most often, the addict doesn't recognize that his or her deepest longing is actually spiritual. We just want an end to the suffering. We can't imagine that anything exists that can actually do that other than death, and perhaps a sufficient amount of drugs which often results in death anyway. To approach an addict touting a "spiritual" answer isn't likely to cause much interest. What appeals to the addict in active addiction is not spirituality, but relief. We emphasize not the spiritual nature of an approach, then, but its effectiveness.

"I haven't had to live like that," is a much more powerful recommendation than, "Let's find God." Much as we have a deep spiritual longing, we most often don't equate that with God. We may see God as judgmental, and we certainly hope God doesn't notice us and our faults.

Nevertheless, a spiritual approach, religious or not, can offer another option, a "third way." Hope must come from *something* that promises to fill the hole in us, the spiritual longing we have, at least as effectively as the drugs did. Without that promise, addiction remains our only choice.

D. J. Mitchell

Chapter Seven
The Need for Hope

I was kicked out of school for drugs at age 17. My parents, dismayed, had me talk to the pastor of my family's church. The pastor told me, "I understand. I've smoked pot." This was an astounding revelation for a pastor in the late 1970s. I know now that he was trying to make a connection with me.

His attempt failed. My reaction was, "If you were like me, you'd be smoking it every day!" He wasn't, therefore he was not like me and couldn't possibly understand me. Rather than helping me to straighten out, as my parents had hoped, the conversation just alienated me further, making me feel different and alone.

Later in my addiction, I preferred opiates. They slowed down my racing thoughts and numbed my body. I would take other depressants, including alcohol, Valium, Quaaludes, and even PCP.

I didn't like amphetamines, because they did the opposite. They made my brain race faster, and I thought too much. But I would take amphetamines if that was all I could find. Even a drug that I didn't like, one that made me miserable, was preferable to the pain I felt when I wasn't high.

Living without drugs was inconceivable for me.

It wasn't until I found others who had been addicted like I was, and who had overcome their addiction through the spiritual program of the Twelve Steps, that I began to believe that it was even possible to live without drugs. Even then, it took some time for me to believe that these well-groomed people had ever really been like me. But my first Twelve Step meeting did give me hope of the possibility of recovery, and I kept coming back long enough for that hope to grow to the point where, out of desperation, I gave the Steps a chance.

As the preceding chapters illustrate, addiction is a complex phenomenon with multiple layers and factors that tend to reinforce each other. At the root is pain from wounds we received in the past.

Physical and behavioral changes mask this hidden influence, often making it invisible. For example, Vic, who used to rob liquor stores to support his habit, was not a typical example of a wounded person. He seemed tough and unshakable. But, as his recovery progressed, he acknowledged childhood abuse and abandonment that had left him untrusting of the world and deeply hurt.

These overlapping layers also combine to convince us that addiction is the only possible answer for us. Most of us have tried to quit many times. Nothing worked. We no longer have any hope for success.

This need for hope is the most important element of any approach to recovery. But it's not just a *message* of hope. Preachers, doctors, and psychologists have promised us we could change, but their solutions haven't worked for us. In the late stages of addiction, any message of hope must include *evidence* to be convincing.

I met Jenna when she was in an inpatient rehabilitation center. She was addicted to crack cocaine, and this was her fifth time in a rehab. This was a nice facility, shiny and modern. Men and women slept in different houses, but mingled during the day, spending more time flirting than thinking about recovery. The staff was entirely professional, psychologists and trained technicians. Not one of them had any personal experience of addiction.

Staff told the clients that the Twelve Steps were essential for recovery, but none of them had actually worked the Steps, and few seemed to have much understanding of them. Instead, the program focused on the same kinds of activities one might find in a behavioral medicine unit: individual and group therapy, light exercise, and yoga. There were no Twelve Step meetings on site, and outside meetings were optional.

Most of the other clients had been through rehab at least once before. Despite the facility's *promise* that change was possible, they demonstrated no real indication that it was. No one, staff or client, provided an example of recovery from addiction. There was no emphasis on a new way of life that could replace the "religion" of addiction.

The facility's promise of hope was, to Jenna, not convincing. Jenna stayed in the 30-day program for two weeks, just long enough to feel better after her last binge. Then she walked away.

I attended a meeting at a facility across town that was very different. The building was old and crowded. All the clients were women. The staff members I met were all in recovery themselves. The speaker at the meeting, an African American, described herself as a "recovering crackhead." As she detailed her dramatic fall into addiction in a charismatic voice, she told of a drug dealer who refused to accept her money and demanded personal services instead.

"You're gonna have to hump a little," she told her audience.

She later described her five years of recovery, and everyone's attention was fixed on her.

The facility was run by people who had struggled with addiction and recovered from it. The speaker, though a different ethnicity from the mostly white and Asian clients, had been to the bottom and come up again. *This* was a message of hope.

*   *   *   *

Of course, not everyone can hear that message, no matter how powerful it is. One of the features of addiction is the self-defense mechanism of denial.

"I'm not really an addict."

"If I could just solve the problems in my life, I'd be okay."

Because addiction becomes a person's purpose for living, our minds will play elaborate tricks to shield us from the truth that addiction is the *cause* of our life problems. This is because addiction is not just a problem, it is a solution.

I once met a man at County General Hospital who was clearly an alcoholic. He'd lost his job, home, and family, and lived in his truck with his dog. He was in the hospital because, while drinking, he'd fallen out of his truck and broken his leg so badly he had to be put in traction. But when I suggested he might have a problem with alcohol, he laughed and told me, "Nah, I just need to find a job."

He'd lost everything to his drinking, but remained convinced that alcohol wasn't his problem.

Denial is most often overcome when the consequences of addiction become too great to bear. But there's no way to know what will trigger this realization. For Margaret, it was the day her pastor confronted her about her pain pill addiction. For Lisa, it was when the state protective services took away her children. Matthew's awakening came when he woke up in the hospital after an overdose. Art's came in jail for some unknown reason—he'd been in jail dozens of times before.

But Mark never did give up his denial. He drank himself onto the street and died behind a building one cold, winter night. He'd been to meetings, but was never really convinced that alcohol was his problem.

Many of us are so afraid of giving up the only meaning we've ever found in life that we will face certain death before we become willing to change.

In this process, hope is essential. Trying to convince an addict that they have a problem is far more likely to succeed if they can see that there just might be an alternative. *Alcoholics Anonymous* describes it this way:

> You say, "Yes, I am willing. But am I to be consigned to a life where I shall be stupid, boring, and glum like some righteous people I know? I know I must get along without liquor, but how can I? Have you a sufficient substitute?" Yes, there is a substitute, and it is vastly more than that...[55]

This promise comes only *after* the book describes the problem of alcoholism and the experience of those who had recovered. For hope to be believable, it must come from someone with credibility. That is, it must come from someone the addict recognizes as having *been* where he or she *is*.

But if the promise is credible, it *does* provide hope—hope the addict has never encountered before.

I use the example of Alcoholics Anonymous because it is widespread and effective, but it is not the only example of successful approaches that can offer hope to those trapped in addiction. I visited a Christian recovery program in Virginia that denied that addiction is a disease. Instead, the founder called addiction the "magnified problem"—masking

---

[55] *Alcoholics Anonymous*, 152.

earlier traumatic wounds that required spiritual and psychological healing.

This approach was quite different from the Twelve Step groups. But its founder had also struggled with addiction, and had spent a significant amount of time incarcerated before starting this ministry thirty years ago.[56] When he says his approach works, people are more likely to believe him because *he's been where they are.* And his program *does* offer hope. Follow-up has shown that more than 80% of those who complete the two-year program stay off drugs for at least five years.[57]

I also visited a residential program in Sri Lanka where a Buddhist monk helps heroin addicts recover using intensive mindfulness meditation. He claims a 90% success rate at one year. Both programs have in common an intensive screening process to choose those candidates who are truly motivated to change, not just avoiding the consequences of their lives of addiction.[58]

*   *   *   *

On the other hand, the Mormon Church has its own Twelve Step meetings, which are very religious in nature.[59] Its

---

[56] "About," The Bridge Ministry
(http://www.bridgeministry.info/about.html, accessed August 9, 2019); William Washington, personal interview, August 8, 2019.

[57] William Washington, personal interview, August 8, 2019.

[58] *Alcoholics Anonymous*, 95, offers similar advice for those sponsoring people in recovery: "If he is not interested in your solution, if he expects you to act only as a banker for his financial difficulties or a nurse for his sprees, you may have to drop him until he changes his mind. This he may do after he gets hurt some more."

[59] Unlike the standard Twelve Steps, in which the 12th Step begins, "Having had a spiritual awakening as a result of these steps," the 12th Step in the Mormon version begins, "Having had a spiritual awakening as a result of the Atonement of Jesus Christ..." "The 12 Steps as Adapted by the Church of Jesus Christ of Latter Day Saints," The Church of Jesus Christ of Latter Day Saints
(https://newsroom.churchofjesuschrist.org/additional-resource/the-12-

meetings are led by church elders, most of whom have never struggled with a substance addiction, and many of whom have never even had a drink because the Mormon Church teaches abstinence with respect to alcohol as well as recreational drugs.

At one meeting I attended, the elderly man leading the meeting insisted, "I understand! When I was young, I once had a drink at a school dance."

I thought, "Seriously? If I could have one drink at a school dance, I wouldn't be here!"

Some people do find help in these meetings. Mike, a habitual marijuana user, was able to quit through this approach. I also know a number of people who got clean and sober in the "Anonymous" programs, and later switched to the Mormon group for religious reasons.

My point is, if you're going to claim to understand addiction, you've got to be convincing. If an addict doesn't hear authenticity, there's no possibility of building trust. They don't hear hope. They hear another person trying to con them.

Alcoholics Anonymous reminds people in recovery that, as folks who have changed our lives, "You can help when no one else can. You can secure their confidence when others fail."[60] The words of a person who has actually recovered from addiction provide more hope than all the psychological or religious approaches combined.

This is not to say that people who aren't addicts can't be helpful. They can, and this will be discussed in a later chapter.

But it's rare that a person who has not recovered from addiction can bring hope to a struggling addict, for the simple reason that the addict sees himself or herself as

steps-as-adapted-by-the-church-of-jesus-christ-of-latter-day-saints, accessed August 9, 2019).
[60] *Alcoholics Anonymous*, 89.

different. The non-addict's experience doesn't seem relevant. Where hope is concerned, having been where they've been is virtually irreplaceable.

Chapter Eight
Where Recovery Begins

I've emphasized trauma and hurt as major underlying factors that drive people to addiction. You might think that the first step in recovery would be to heal those old wounds.

That isn't the case. When we first get clean and sober, the greatest challenge we face is simply this: what do we do each day?

Our life in addiction may have been chaotic, but it was ordered by a single, overpowering purpose: to obtain and use more drugs. We *knew* what our purpose was. Every action we took in a day was an attempt to achieve that purpose.

Without that purpose, what do we do, and why do we do it? "Normal" people will tell us to get a job, rent an apartment, and perhaps go to church. But why? Aside from supporting necessary daily nutrition, which many of us had neglected during our addiction, what is the purpose of work? Yes, we need a place to stay, but what do we do there besides eat and sleep?

And then there's that hole in us, of which we are acutely aware every moment, especially when we have nothing to do. The "triggers" that push us to the act of drinking or using are nearly always present, but we are most vulnerable to them when we have nothing to distract us from them.[61]

---

[61] "Triggers" are a tricky subject. Yes, there are certain conditions which are more likely to encourage us to drink or use. At the same time, someone who wants to or is accustomed to drink and use doesn't need a trigger. For me in my addiction, the sun rising or setting was a trigger. An overemphasis on triggers distracts us from the need to develop healthy

Ironically, in the absence of new solutions, even successes and joy can return us to old behaviors. Our old patterns combined with our misplaced love predispose us to drinking or using to celebrate good times as well as to tolerate bad times.

Assuming that we have found sufficient hope to get us to start the recovery process, and that we have some support from people who know what it's like to give up a substance addiction, the next thing we need is something to keep us occupied. This is where Twelve Step programs excel, especially in major cities where there's a meeting at almost any time of day. But meetings are not the only possibility. Some groups maintain clubhouses that are open all day, and sometimes all night.

When I was newly clean, people would insist that I join them at a coffee shop after the meeting. Others gave me their phone number and told me to call any time, day or night. I didn't believe they meant it, but about 3:00 in the morning I found my thoughts spinning out of control and I called one of these men.[62] He took my call and happily talked me through it—because when he was new, he'd been in a similar situation.

This camaraderie, this mutual support, is not found in many places other than Twelve Step meetings. Try calling your boss, doctor, or pastor at 3:00 am!

A group of newly recovering people naturally formed, and I found myself going to the beach, to movies (which I hadn't done in almost a decade), and even rock concerts with them. This provided not only constant activity, but also support in our recovery. We'd talk about the Steps, our challenges, and our relationship with our sponsor. If someone seemed in

---

approaches to life that allow us to weather the triggers we encounter.

[62] As mentioned previously, it is customary in Twelve Step groups for men to work with men and women to work with women.

danger of returning to active addiction, we'd talk them through it.

One man in our group always brought the book *Alcoholics Anonymous* with him. As we sat on the beach enjoying the sun and the scenery, he'd open the book and begin reading a page at random. At the time, we found this a little annoying. In hindsight, it helped keep us focused.

Alex found another source for this type of needed structure: he got clean and sober in a church. This was an unusual church. The pastor had struggled with addiction. The worship band played Christian heavy metal music. And the church had activities and small groups to ensure that its members had access to the necessary support.

Most churches aren't oriented toward the needs of people in recovery. They meet once a week for an hour or so, and perhaps there's a Bible study during the week. This doesn't fill the need of a newly clean addict trying to adopt a new life, who struggles with what to do *every day*, and sometimes minute by minute.

This is also the failure of the typical expectation of just returning someone to "normal" life. We get a job, at which we're surrounded by "normal" people who have no idea what we're going through. We go home to an empty apartment at night and sit with no company other than swirling thoughts and perhaps the television, bored and restless with no one to talk to, the hole in our gut aching and demanding attention.

That model is doomed to fail. An addict does not suddenly start thinking healthy thoughts just because he or she stops using drugs. In moments of crisis, without real alternatives, those unhealthy thoughts provide the only solution available: return to old behaviors.

This need for activity is temporary. As recovery progresses, we also need to learn to be comfortable in our own skin. But in those first few weeks or months of being clean, structure is essential.

There needs to be more to our new routine than just staying busy. Otherwise, we're replacing one addiction, the substance, with another: activity. This is not at all unusual. We have a hole that needs to be filled, and unless we find another way to fill it, we'll find a different addiction. It may be sex, money, work, eating, or golf. Kent Dunnington observes, "As soon as one addictive desire is banished from the scene, another appears."[63] We will find *something* to cover up that hole for at least a moment.

Brian is a good example. He started as a moderate drinker, but by the time he was thirty he drank all day and all night. He couldn't work, was abusive to his family, and his health was failing. If he tried to stop drinking, he experienced seizures because he was so physically addicted. Eventually, he consented to be hospitalized. He was successfully detoxed from alcohol, and he attended a few Twelve Step meetings but decided they weren't for him. Instead, he threw himself into his work.

Brian has now been sober more than ten years. He still works 60 hours a week, not because he has to, but because it keeps him busy. He switched from an addiction to alcohol to an addiction to work.

It's not uncommon for people early in recovery to engage in promiscuity. For one thing, an addict deep in their addiction is not very attractive and, even if the opportunity presents itself, men may not be able to perform because of the drugs. Once off the drugs, they *can*, and they have *opportunity*. They want to feel attractive, liked, even loved. Often this is a phase, but it can develop into a replacement addiction.

---

[63] Dunnington, 50.

A life of addiction is a *habit* in the classical sense: our actions stem from an "internal disposition" to use drugs. This is not something we're born with, but something that develops as our addiction satisfies our internal needs. That need is to fill the hole. Our actions reflect this need. In order to change, we need new actions *and* another solution for the hole in us.

Our habit is deeply ingrained, but not unchangeable. We change these habits by practicing new habits.[64] But we also change our habits by finding a new purpose for life. We have to find something new to love, besides the drug.[65] This only makes sense: if we want to adopt new habits, we have to have a good reason for taking these new actions. Otherwise, we will only be motivated to take actions that feel good, and that tends to lead us into another addiction.

*　　　*　　　*　　　*

Why must we love something? It's what gives us purpose. *Everyone* loves something. But, as James K. A. Smith observes, what we love may not be what we think we love. We can tell what we really love by our actions.[66]

Susan swore that she loved her son above all else. But she would often abandon him to go drinking. Her *actions* indicated that she loved alcohol more than she loved her son.

The question is not whether we must love something, but *what* we should love. We should choose something that fills that spiritual need for purpose. The object of our love needs to be something greater than ourselves. For most people in our society, that means some conception of God.

It is true that the Twelve Step programs don't tell us what to believe. They intentionally choose the language of

---

[64] Smith, 17-19.
[65] Ibid., 32.
[66] Smith, 12, 32.

"higher power" and "God as we understood God." A pastor recently asked me to confirm that in these programs, you can choose a telephone pole as your higher power.

Technically that is true: you can choose a telephone pole or a lawnmower to be your higher power. But that isn't going to work. If, as the Twelve Step programs suggest, we stay clean and sober through power (or at least motivation) given to us by our higher power, then our higher power must be able to give us power or motivation. Can a telephone pole do that? Can we "Turn our will and our lives over to the care of" a lawnmower, as the 3rd Step suggests? I can't categorically rule it out, but it's difficult to see how such a conception would serve a person for any length of time.

We must choose a higher power that is worthy to serve as the object of our love. Why would one pledge devotion to an inanimate object?

Doug, the militant atheist mentioned earlier, chose the betterment of society, which was the ancient Greek philosopher Aristotle's ideal goal. Aristotle called it *eudemonia*, human flourishing.

During my years of agnosticism, my higher power was the Twelve Step program itself. It guided my life, and I was committed to practicing it and carrying it to others who suffered from addiction.

I have met Buddhists whose commitment was to the Buddha's Eightfold Path, a model for living that Buddhists believe will lead to Enlightenment. Buddhism doesn't recognize a God, but it does teach compassion for all life and thus is not only a personal spiritual journey.[67]

Christianity, as described in the New Testament, with its call to daily discipleship and its promise of the Holy Spirit, is

---

[67] See for example Caiti Schroering, "Joanna Macy, Buddhism, and Power for Social Change," *Denison Journal of Religion* 2010:9. Macy is one of the foremost scholars on "engaged" Buddhism, as reflected in the practices of Thich Nhat Hanh and A. T. Ariyaratne.

uniquely suited for addicts in recovery. Unfortunately, many addicts have had painful experiences with people who claimed to be Christians but who had little understanding of addiction.

I've been to many churches that claimed that addiction could be solved if we "just believe." In my agnostic years, I didn't know how to believe. Was there some switch I could flip to suddenly accept something I had not accepted before, without new evidence or experience? If there was such a switch, I couldn't find it.

But more than that, religious approaches often failed to address what we *do* once we come to believe. Belief and action are equally important for recovery. As addicts we need more than just a new belief system. We need a new way of life. And we need to practice that way of life every day.

*　　　*　　　*　　　*

To begin our recovery, we must have a new structure for our lives that fills the empty spaces formerly occupied with our life-consuming quest for drugs. The ideal structure will be built around activities that become a habit, just as seeking and using drugs was a habit. The new structure must build and reinforce positive, life-affirming actions. It will orient us toward a new focus for our love to replace the drug we formerly worshipped. And that focus must be substantial enough to become a purpose for our lives that is not just another addiction that masks our wounds.

Kent Dunnington describes this well: "[T]he life of recovery is a life of rehabituation rather than merely a life of repetition of acts of abstinence."[68] It matters not just *whether* we find an alternative to our addiction, but *what* that alternative is. Money won't heal us, nor will a telephone pole.

---

[68] Dunnington, 79.

Workaholism, promiscuity, overeating, or any other replacement addiction may not land us in jail or cause us to overdose, but it will continue our pattern of seeking to fill the hole inside us with things or behaviors. All of these will keep us self-centered and broken.

We don't begin the recovery process with healing. But we will need to heal. The object of our love must be sufficient to promote healing, not prevent it. We need to find a higher power that doesn't just mask our pain, but which can actually help us to heal the wounds that drove us to seek pain relief in the first place.

CHAPTER NINE
HEALING THE RIFT

When we are practicing our addiction, the physical disease aspect of addiction is the most prominent. We drink and use, and once we start we can't stop because of an overpowering physical craving for more. Many of us never stop long enough for that craving to cease.

But, as argued previously, this is not the primary problem. The physical disease would be irrelevant if we never took that first drink or drug. Most often, we do so because we are seeking relief from pain. For recovery to be successful in the long term, we have to heal the causes of that pain.

Healing occurs at several levels, physical, psychological, and spiritual. And there are many different means of healing. Those who describe addiction as a physical disease focus particularly on physical separation from the drug, and healing of the damage addiction causes to the body.

Addiction does ravage the body. Jim, a heroin addict for many years, finally got clean in a Twelve Step program, but died four months later of a heart attack. He was 32 years old.

Lance had been drinking for thirty years when he got sober. But he'd already damaged his liver beyond repair and died within a year.

Alice died of a heart attack at age 40 when, after almost a year of staying off drugs, she decided to try it just once more.

Often the damage is not fatal. Juan had alcoholic paralysis in one leg when he got sober, and it took time and medical attention for him to be able to walk normally.

Walt came into a Twelve Step program with "wet brain," a form of brain damage caused by alcohol abuse. It is considered irreversible. Those who knew Walt said he'd been nearly comatose when he'd gotten sober. Yet when I met him, years later, Walt had regained the capacity to think and speak.

The physical damage of addiction is the most critical to deal with, and often heals relatively quickly. But it's the unseen psychological and spiritual damage that often causes us the most trouble in our recovery. We feel different, alienated from society, and, depending on our nature, either unworthy of recovery because of our past failures or angry at society for what we perceive it has done to us—perhaps even both at the same time. We have secrets we're sure would destroy us if they were discovered. We're angry at specific people in our lives, and we carry the guilt of the things we have done.

We carry these problems close to the surface, and they can negatively impact our recovery pretty quickly if we ignore them. They must be addressed if we are to be successful.

* * * *

It is appropriate to talk here about responsibility. A major criticism of the "disease model" of addiction is that it permits the addict to avoid responsibility for his or her actions.[69] Kent Dunnington argues that if a person truly cannot recover, then they can't be held responsible—but if a person does

---

[69] For example, Eric Racine, Sebastian Sadler, and Alice Escande, "Free Will and the Brain Disease Model of Addiction: The Not So Seductive Allure of Neuroscience and Its Modest Impact on the Attribution of Free Will to People with an Addiction," *Front. Psychol.*, 01 Nov 2017, https://doi.org/10.3389/fpsyg.2017.01850, have shown that increased education and knowledge of neuroscience correspond with reduced belief that addicts and alcoholics have free will in their actions. The authors argue that if an addict does not have free will, logically he or she cannot be held responsible for their actions.

eventually recover, even after years of trying, then their addiction was in some way voluntary.[70]

While I disagree with Dunnington's logic, his conclusion about responsibility is not wrong. An analogy might be with a person who is blind. That is a condition that the person has no control over. But if the blind person attempts to drive his or her car, *that action* is the result of poor judgment, and despite the person's handicap, he or she is liable for the consequences.

"I couldn't see the pedestrian," is not a sufficient defense.

It is absurd to argue that it was the person's blindness, rather than the decision to operate a motor vehicle, that caused the incident.

Likewise, even if addiction is a state beyond our control, we make choices about *how* to support our habit. We can argue that we cannot stop using drugs. We cannot argue that robbing a liquor store was an unavoidable way to do so.

Whether or not addiction is a disease—or, as this book argues, even if it has some characteristics of a disease—the addict must be fully responsible for *actions* taken during

---

[70] Dunnington, 39-41. Here Dunnington uses Aristotle's three categories of the "self-indulgent," the "incontinent" and the "morbid" addict. The self-indulgent addict practices addiction because he or she "wishes to engage in addictive action" (41). Both of the latter categories are people who do not wish to engage in such action, the difference being that the incontinent addict is able to recover while the morbid addict is not. However, in actual practice these two categories are less than useful. The distinction is made by whether the person recovers before they die. But if a teenager fatally overdoses, cutting their life short, is that a fair indication that he or she was a morbid addict? Conversely, if a long-term addict struggles but fails to recover, then later in life has a spiritual experience, for example, that renders them able to recover, can we attribute the prior behavior as incontinent? Here I would note that Aristotle, not being Christian, lacked an important concept that later thinkers embraced: grace. (See, for example, Augustine, "On Grace and Free Will" (http://www.newadvent.org/fathers/1510.htm, accessed August 12, 2019), IV.1.) Many recovering addicts, including myself, attribute their recovery to the grace of God—not that our own actions toward recovery were unnecessary, but that they were insufficient.

addiction. To say otherwise equates the condition of addiction with the choices made, which is a logical fallacy.

Relieving the addict of responsibility for the consequences of his or her actions also continues the rift between the addict and society. But we *must* clean the slate if we are to be reconciled to the world.

Despite criticism of the Twelve Step programs on this matter, these programs *do* insist that the addict is responsible for his or her actions. *Alcoholics Anonymous* says, with respect to making amends, "Now we go out to our fellows and repair the damage done in the past. We attempt to sweep away the debris that has accumulated out of our effort to live on self-will and run the show ourselves."[71]

But AA doesn't see alcohol as the primary problem. It says succinctly, "Our liquor was but a symptom." As it observes, "These observations [about the physical craving during drinking] would be academic and pointless if our friend never took the first drink..."[72] Rather, AA considers the primary malady to be spiritual.

This presents a problem for the medical community, which tends to dismiss spiritual matters, or to lump them into psychology.[73] AA does recognize that "there is no such thing as making a normal drinker out of an alcoholic."[74] We *are* physically different. Once we start drinking or using, we can't stop. But, so long as we avoid taking that first one, this difference need not keep us apart from society.

But the rifts resulting from our life in addiction must be healed. Again, this is where the Twelve Step programs excel. The Twelve Steps are intended to address precisely these issues that make us feel separate from those around us.

---

[71] *Alcoholics Anonymous*, 76.

[72] *Alcoholics Anonymous*, 64, 23.

[73] This divergence between the Twelve Step programs and medical/psychological approaches to recovery suggests that there is no unified "recovery community," as some critics suggest.

[74] Ibid., 31.

For example, the Fourth Step has the participant make "a searching and fearless moral inventory of ourselves." The description of this step in *Alcoholics Anonymous* gives the most space to resentments, the feeling that others have wronged us. We list the people we resent, something most addicts are happy to do. But then we analyze how the actions of the other person affect us. Do they threaten our self esteem, our financial health, or even our freedom? Then comes the most critical part: reflecting on the role we ourselves had in the interaction.[75]

Our own part can be elusive, especially for an alcoholic or addict whose brain goes to great lengths to defend his or her actions. Larry, for example, told me he resented a former friend because the friend denigrated Larry's character to others. As we discussed the matter, Larry finally admitted that he had stolen from that friend. But in Larry's mind, the two events were unrelated until he consciously connected them.

There are also resentments in which we did not do anything to trigger the other person's action. Someone may have harmed us without provocation.

Stan resented a close friend because that friend was supposed to take care of his girlfriend while Stan was in jail. The friend seduced her and she became his girlfriend instead. Clearly Stan had *expectations* that were not met. It's amazing how often addicts expect their fellow addicts to adhere to some code of honor that they themselves don't follow!

But sometimes the expectations are reasonable. We expect our boss to pay us on time. We expect our parents to love and care for us. We expect religious leaders not to abuse us. If these expectations aren't met, we become angry and resentful. This anger may be entirely justified. But rather

---

[75] Ibid., 59, 63-67.

than working through it, we bury it and carry it with us. For addicts, these lingering resentments can be fatal.[76]

Other parts of this inventory process include listing our fears and recognizing the limits of our self reliance. We analyze our relationships, especially intimate relationships, and recognize our selfishness. And we list those secrets we were never going to tell anyone.[77]

*   *   *   *

The Fifth Step is to share this inventory with a trustworthy person, usually a sponsor, the person whom the participant chooses to help them work the Steps. This sharing process is critical. The inventory contains thoughts, behaviors, and actions that the person may never have admitted to another person. They are secrets. Every secret serves to separate us from others with fear of discovery. The act of sharing our secrets with even just one person removes their power.

Confidentiality is of course essential. No one would share any important secret if they couldn't rely on the listener to keep such things confidential. The bigger the secret, the greater the shame and fear of discovery, and the more likelihood that the person will return to their addiction. Confidentiality saves lives.

Most people haven't done anything truly remarkable, but because their actions are secret they seem like the worst sins in the world. Most addicts have stolen, lied, and engaged in inappropriate sexual behavior. But no matter how bad or insignificant their transgressions, they simply cannot recover while these remain secret.

Some of these actions are disturbing. Over the years, men have reported to me all manner of sins, including murder, rape, incest, bestiality, sexual abuse (both giving

---

[76] Ibid., 66.
[77] Ibid., 67-70.

and receiving), and child abuse.[78] There's a saying in the Twelve Step programs: "If there's a word for it, someone has done it before." Yet we promise absolute confidentiality, even when we are told of serious crimes.

This may seem unreasonable. These days, absolute confidentiality has fallen out of favor in many segments of society, including church and the workplace. Many people believe that a major transgression admitted in any context should be reported.

The Twelve Step situation is significantly different for two reasons. First, people's lives are at stake. Without the process of confession in a trustworthy relationship, they may very well die of their addiction.

But more importantly, a person has to be pretty serious about recovery to share these kinds of details with another person. It could be described as an act of desperation by someone who knows they can't get better unless they do it. These are not people seeking absolution for their sins—the Twelve Steps don't offer that.

In fact, Step Nine of the process requires that the participant make amends for their transgressions as best they can. In short, as one old-timer put it, they pay back the money. This, too, is a critical step. We do our best to clean up the messes we made, which sets us right with the world.

There are obviously actions that can't be undone. I once spoke with a man who, before he had gotten clean and sober, had killed people for a gang. At the time of our conversation, he'd been in recovery for over thirty years. He told me that he could have turned himself in and spent a decade on death row, but in prayer he had decided that such a course would do little to undo what he had done. Instead, he'd spent the past thirty years intentionally trying to do for people what he wished he could do for the people he'd killed. He gave away

---

[78] By tradition, and for practical reasons, the general rule in Twelve Step programs is that men work with men and women work with women.

his money and his time in an effort to put back into the world what he had taken, knowing that no amount of effort would ever fully accomplish that.

Which is the better answer, death row or a life of penitence? Surely we could debate that. Just as surely, there's something to be said about reconciliation rather than punishment.

I've now been clean and sober more than 35 years. I still feel the weight of the lives I destroyed when I talked people into using drugs. The shame never goes away. And it motivates me to reach out to those suffering at every opportunity.

I don't get to say, "I'm too busy," or "I'm too tired." I owe a debt that can never be repaid, but I will do my best anyway.

Maybe some would say I should have been sent to prison instead. That would have cost the taxpayers nearly a million dollars over these years, and I wouldn't have been able to help anyone.

The premise of recovery is that people clean up their old lives, and begin new and productive lives. The New Testament might phrase it this way: "If anyone is in Christ, he is a new creation" (2 Corinthians 5:17).

The Twelve Step programs don't have a monopoly on this process. In fact, they adopted the practice from a Christian discipleship group called the Oxford Group back in the 1930s.[79] Confession and restitution are part of Christianity and nearly every other world religion.[80] They are beneficial for anyone. But for addicts who wish to recover, they are

---

[79] Dick B., *Design for Living: The Oxford Group's Contribution to Early A.A.*, San Rafael, CA: Paradise Research Publications, 1995, 76, 83; James Stanley Bezzant, "'The Groups,'" *Modern Churchman* 21 (10), 1932: 537–546. https://hartzler.emu.edu/login?url=https://search-ebscohost-com.hartzler.emu.edu/login.aspx?direct=true&db=lsdar&AN=ATLA0001779031&site=ehost-live&scope=site, 537-538.

essential for healing the rift we perceive between us and the world around us.

---

[80] See for example James 5:16, Numbers 5:5-7, Quran 66:8, Triskandharma Sutra, Bodhicaryāvatāra 2, Taittiriya Samhita 5.3.12.1, etc.

CHAPTER TEN
FINDING PURPOSE

The typical addict is extremely self-centered. Everything in his or her life revolves around the self, and specifically trying to fill the hole inside. Though we may have moments of charity and care for others, our inward disposition is to care for our wounded selves. We often can't see beyond our own needs. It is this worldview that justifies the lies, theft, and manipulation that characterize so many of our lives while in addiction.

Recovery demands a new outlook. The answer to filling the hole inside us cannot be found inside us, nor in anything we might obtain through selfish effort. The quest for money, comfort, and even love can become an addiction in itself if our only object of concern is our own comfort. As James K. A. Smith writes, "The habits we've acquired shape how we perceive the world, which in turn disposes us to act in certain ways."[81] If relieving our own pain is our only focus, we will continue to act in addictive ways, despite the fact that the best we have ever achieved is temporary relief.

It doesn't help that our society increasingly values self-promotion to the exclusion of helping others. Kent Dunnington writes, "[L]ate modern capitalism provides consumers with the opportunity to pursue 'value' in the absence of any shared commitment to the good."[82] We're taught to seek our own benefit, our own comfort, and to let others worry about theirs. This is not a satisfactory purpose

---

[81] Smith, 36.
[82] Dunnington, 112.

for life. In fact, Dunnington argues, "[C]onsumerism is an expression of the wish to be distracted from the frightening prospect that we do not really know what is worthwhile."[83]

Dunnington sees addiction as a reaction against the lack of purpose present in our society, the complete pluralism that demands that *we* discover for ourselves what is worthwhile. In the face of uncertainty about why we're here, addiction provides an ordering principle for life. It provides a purpose, flawed as that purpose may be. He quotes Ann Marlow: "Heroin is a stand-in, a stop-gap, a mask, for what we believe is missing."[84]

What's missing is a purpose that is bigger than us. We're all going somewhere; the purpose is our destination. Without a purpose, we're driving without a destination. So what is worthwhile, and how do we discover what that is? Usually we need guidance. We can't figure out what is worthwhile on our own. That's the fallacy of our pluralistic culture.

Alcoholics Anonymous gives a broad statement of purpose when it says, "Your job now is to be at the place where you can be of maximum helpfulness to others..."[85] It becomes more specific in suggesting that our purpose as people in recovery from addiction is to be of service specifically to other people struggling as we were.[86] Experience and the success of Twelve Step programs suggests that this is indeed a sufficient purpose for life.

But it's not the only possibility. Doug, the one-time atheist, saw the betterment of society as his purpose. The New Testament charges followers of Jesus to "Proclaim the good news... cure the sick, raise the dead, cleanse the lepers, cast out demons... give without payment" (Matthew 10:7-8).

---

[83] Ibid.

[84] Ann Marlow, *How to Stop Time: Heroin from A to Z* (New York: Basic Books, 1999), 155, quoted in Dunnington, 108.

[85] *Alcoholics Anonymous*, 102.

[86] Ibid., 60, 89, etc.

This theme of service to others is central to a purpose sufficient to guide our lives *and fill the hole* that we have felt as long as we can remember.

This may seem like a paradox. By selflessly helping others, we help ourselves. Selflessness seems to be selfish. And in the beginning, our motives are unlikely to be pure. We do indeed help others because we want something, namely relief from our pain. But over time, helping others becomes our inward disposition, replacing addictive behavior, because we have found a purpose that really *does* fill the hole. When the hole is filled, we stop craving relief. We begin to help others not for any reward, but because we realize it is the right thing to do. It becomes a way of life—even when it's inconvenient, or detrimental to our immediate interests.

For most addicts, this is new behavior. There are exceptions. Toward the end of my active addiction, when I was in bad shape, Fran and Jack, both addicts themselves, fed me and gave me odd jobs for money and drugs. They were people with compassion, despite the addiction that later took both their lives.

But most of us were pretty selfish. We did nothing that didn't give us some benefit. As we enter recovery, this attitude doesn't change unless we make a determined effort to change it.

*   *   *   *

There are many models for shifting our attention to others. *Alcoholics Anonymous* says, "Practical experience shows that nothing will so much insure immunity from drinking as intensive work with other alcoholics... Life will take on new meaning."[87] Similarly, Jesus counsels us, "Whoever tries to save his life will lose it..." (Luke 17:33). His teaching was

------

[87] Ibid., 89.

meant for everyone, but applies particularly well to addicts. Self-centeredness, for an addict, will kill us. Only by expanding our horizons to the suffering of others can we begin to be healed.

There is a multitude of ways to be of service. Working with other addicts and alcoholics is one that many follow, both in Twelve Step programs and outside of them. We are uniquely suited to that work. But some choose overseas or urban missions, where they work with those who are economically challenged. Others go into medicine or other healing arts. Some work for change within the political system. Jake now manages a homeless shelter. Susan practices spiritual healing. Ted brings Twelve Step meetings into prisons. I became a minister.

A wise man named Bert, who has since passed away after many years in recovery, said, "When I'm thinking about you, I'm not thinking about me." That profoundly simple statement holds much truth for addicts. Our selfishness leads us back into addiction. Thinking of others helps keep us *out* of addiction.

We don't do this naturally. Like our daily habits, we need to *practice* caring for others. And we usually need guidance and encouragement.

When I was new in recovery, every time someone was moving my sponsor insisted that I go help them. Eventually this became a habit. It was a small thing, but it began to teach me to put the needs of others ahead of my own desire to stay home, be comfortable, and isolate.

Tim's sponsor suggested that he serve food at a soup kitchen once a week. Bob used to let alcoholics stay at his house for a few days at a time. Sandy spent an afternoon each week sitting with and listening to elderly people at a nursing home. Frank was instructed by his sponsor to take struggling alcoholics to meetings in his brand new Cadillac.

He often talked about the irony of becoming willing to pick up homeless men who hadn't showered, or people who were vomiting in alcohol withdrawal, in the car he'd bought to make himself feel better.

Each of these was an exercise in selflessness, a small willingness to be of service. It was a first step, and encouraged by their sponsor. But over time it became a habit, and expanded to change the person's attitude from selfish to service. This is how we find new purpose for life. And it's the first step in filling the hole in us that's been there as long as we can remember.

D. J. Mitchell

CHAPTER ELEVEN
HEALING THE WOUNDS

The rifts that separate us from society are among the most problematic issues that prevent us from successfully recovering. They are close to the surface and tend to manifest fairly quickly. But they are by no means the only pain we carry. We have been wounded both psychologically and spiritually. In order to find long-term recovery these, too, need attention. And the more we heal, the better and more resilient our recovery will be. But this usually takes place after a period of stable recovery, when we have regained the ability to focus and reflect.

Healing childhood traumas may mean reliving those traumas as we acknowledge their details and their impact on our lives. This generally is not something that should be attempted without professional help, nor without a solid foundation in recovery. Even with professional help, the process can cause emotional upheaval, challenges to existing relationships, questions of faith, and even crises of identity.

I first sought help with trauma when I had 14 years in recovery, after a trip to do volunteer work exposed me to unexpected violence. When I came home from the trip, I felt like my skin had disappeared and there was nothing between my inner pain and the world outside. I couldn't work, had nightmares every night, and could barely talk to people about what had happened.

The first therapist I worked with helped me review my life for previous traumas. That's when I identified the incident of abuse by my cousin. But there were other traumas I hadn't recognized. My best friend moved away when I was five years old. At eight, I witnessed a fatal bicycle accident. At ten, I lost another best friend. At twelve, the school bully would beat me up regularly. At fourteen, I witnessed a friend almost losing his leg in another bicycle accident.

I had experienced multiple traumas that my parents and teachers hadn't known about, or hadn't recognized. I was predisposed to PTSD because I already had it. That's why the incident I experienced as an adult affected me perhaps more than it might have affected someone else. And, more than ten years in recovery, I no longer had the option of self-medicating.

It took years of work with therapists of different specialties in order to heal from all that. I did talk therapy, directed journaling, eye movement desensitization and reprocessing (EMDR), dialectical behavior therapy (DBT), and other forms of healing. It took time, and it took work. But healing happened.

I've met people in recovery from addiction whose early childhood traumas have caused psychotic episodes, dissociative disorders, and severe depression.[88] When these are caused by old traumas, temporary fixes like medication can be helpful, depending on the circumstances. But healing those wounds is the only way to fully recover.

*   *   *   *

We have also experienced spiritual wounds. Some of these have been relational. We ceased to trust God, and this led us to rely only on ourselves. We judged a religion by the behavior of some of its followers. Or we decided that the evidence of our miserable lives was sufficient to prove that

---

[88] I do not intend to claim that trauma is the only cause of such problems. It is not. But it is a possible cause that is sometimes overlooked.

there was no God, no purpose, and no meaning apart from what we could do for ourselves.

There are also other types of spiritual problems. Even after we have confessed our misdeeds and made amends or restitution, we may feel deep guilt or shame about some of the things we've done or not done, especially those things that can't really be set right. We may feel unworthy or even self-destructive. Psychology can offer some help, but ultimately, in many instances, this is a spiritual problem. Every religion, every cultural manifestation of religion, and nearly every spiritual path offers some means of redemption.

Other problems include the feeling (and sometimes the reality) of being cursed, or even becoming aware of the presence of evil within us.

There are many approaches to these problems, most often specific to each individual religion. Christianity, for example, has pastoral counseling, spiritual direction, forms of prayer therapy, Gestalt Pastoral Care, healing ministries, and even deliverance from spirits. Most other religions have something comparable. These experts in spiritual and religious matters can be extremely helpful with the healing process.

But healing often requires more than one approach.

Jay, for example, became a Christian as a teenager. But later, he became addicted to drugs. He believed that evil spirits were the cause of his inability to leave drugs alone, and he sought help from a deliverance ministry. A team of three people, over two hours-long sessions, helped him with the spirits that tormented him. During that process, Jay learned that one of the causes of his addiction was abuse from an uncle his family had lived with when he was a child.

The ministers told Jay that, in order to fully heal, he would need first of all to engage in some kind of spiritual work, such as the Twelve Steps—which Jay knew of through a Christian recovery program he'd attended. And he would need to get psychological help for his childhood trauma.

Unfortunately, Jay believed that going to church each week would be enough to maintain his recovery. It wasn't. The church Jay attended believed strongly in the healing power of Christ. But they had no experience in addiction or trauma work. Jay stayed clean several months, but later relapsed and returned to drug use.

Barbara was clean for several months when I met her. She insisted that she didn't have any spiritual problems that church couldn't fix. But she later confessed that she'd been sexually abused as a child, and that she, too, sometimes felt like there were spirits affecting her thinking. She didn't seek help, and although she stayed clean, she lost her marriage as she became more paranoid and controlling.

Felix came into recovery after living in his car for several months. He suffered from severe depression and feelings of unworthiness. He had been chronically emotionally abused by his father as a child, and this had given him a desire for perfection that he could never live up to.

He began working with several spiritual healers, and seemed to be making progress. But his experiences at a church that did not understand people in recovery led him to abandon religion as a resource. He returned to regular marijuana use, and continues to move from job to job, struggling to survive.

One of the challenges for people with substance addiction is that most churches *don't* really understand addiction. Some church members are even afraid of what the church would look like, or how it would be perceived, if addicts began to fill its membership.[89]

---

[89] One survey found that 70% of respondents saw lack of knowledge as the greatest barrier to church effectiveness in helping addicts—they didn't know how. But 30% cited Negative Perception (they don't want to attract people who are different from them), and 26% cited Fear (they are afraid of how it would change the church). These add up to more than 100%

But beyond the lack of understanding, attending church once a week, while it may be sufficient for many people, cannot fill the void left by our former "religion" of addiction, with its daily practice and focus. Addicts need more. In Christianity, we would call it daily discipleship.

The Twelve Steps provide this. There are some religion-based programs that do, but not many.

Christianity has the potential to be extremely effective in helping addicts recover, but this potential has not been realized. In conversations with pastors who have no experience in addiction, and with those who do because they have experienced it, I have come to believe that creating such opportunities will need to come from recovering addicts themselves. It seems difficult for non-addicts to grasp the necessity for daily worship to replace the role the substance once had as the center of our lives.

The same appears to be true in other religions as well. All have some form of daily practice that goes beyond what the typical participant adopts. Small groups of addicts can create for each other a religious support community that the Church as whole (or other religious body) generally cannot provide.

Spiritual healing is an important part of the recovery process, but it is not the only part. We should never discount the role of qualified therapists and psychologists, nor of medical doctors. Addiction damages us on many levels, and healing must also happen on many levels. But this takes time. We should also be careful not to have unreasonable expectations. The damage of years of trauma and addiction may take years or even decades to heal. And it requires a stable foundation of recovery in order to make progress.

---

because more than one answer was allowed. D. J. Mitchell, "Congregational Survey," Eastern Mennonite Seminary (unpublished), February 28, 2019.

Chapter Twelve
What Is Treatment?

Jenna was in her fifth round at a treatment facility when I met her. She dropped out before the end of the program and went back to using drugs.

Nate got clean and sober the first time he went to treatment and never used again.

Ben was sentenced to treatment by the court after his fifth conviction for DUI. He went to avoid prison, yet he got clean and stayed clean for many years.

Vivian had a spiritual experience after an alcoholic binge, attended Twelve Step meetings and never drank again.

Dan found sobriety in a church run by a pastor in recovery.

Al got sober through Twelve Step meetings while in prison for vehicular manslaughter.

Vern failed at treatment facilities and methadone clinics for years, but after doing some time in jail and living in his car for a year, he finally got clean in a Twelve Step program.

Treatment takes many forms, and has varying rates of success. But, whether an expensive rehab facility, a publicly funded treatment center, a church-based support group, or a cost-free Twelve Step meeting, some form of support is usually necessary to help us get out and stay out of our addiction. The reason is simple: If we knew how to stay clean and sober without treatment, if we could envision a way of life sufficient to replace addiction, we would have given up drugs already.

Treatment for drug and alcohol addiction is big business in the United States. In 2017, nearly three million people underwent treatment.[90] It's estimated that Americans spend $30-35 billion a year attending rehabilitation centers for drug and alcohol abuse.

That doesn't include the nation's largest single "treatment" system: prison. According to researchers Wendy Sawyer and Peter Wagner, nearly half of all federal prisoners, about 100,000 people, are incarcerated for nonviolent drug offenses.[91] It's estimated that half a million nonviolent drug offenders are incarcerated in state and local prison systems.[92] At an estimated $30,000 per prisoner per year, that's another $15 billion expense that falls to the taxpayers.

In 2016, some 168,000 people on parole or probation were returned behind bars not because they committed a new crime but because of technical violations such as staying out past curfew. Sawyer and Wagner argue that the justice system is structured to promote failure, not to reward success.[93]

It's worth noting that those who go through treatment are more likely to be white (about 80%). Those who go to

---

[90] Bose, Table 5.10A.

[91] "What America Spends on Drug Addictions," Addiction-Resources.com, 2005 (https://www.addiction-treatment.com/in-depth/what-america-spends-on-drug-addictions/, accessed August 14, 2019). There are many more recent estimates on what Americans spend on the substances themselves, but I was unable to find a more current estimate of the cost of rehab. Gabrielle Glaser, "The Irrationality of Alcoholics Anonymous," *Atlantic* Feb 2015 (https://www.theatlantic.com/magazine/archive/2015/04/the-irrationality-of-alcoholics-anonymous/386255/, accessed August 15, 2019). "Offenses," Federal Bureau of Prisons, Aug 9, 2019 (https://www.bop.gov/about/statistics/statistics_inmate_offenses.jsp, accessed August 14, 2019).

[92] Wendy Sawyer and Peter Wagner, "Mass Incarceration: The Whole Pie 2020," Prison Policy Initiative, March 24, 2020 (https://www.prisonpolicy.org/reports/pie2020.html, accessed May 15, 2020).

[93] Ibid.

prison are more likely not to be white (about 70%). The rate of addiction does vary slightly between races, but perhaps not as expected. Of the three most populous races, whites lead in substance abuse problems with 7.7%. Blacks have a rate of 6.8%, and 6.6% of Hispanics struggle with substance abuse.[94] Yet blacks are six times more likely to be incarcerated for drug offenses than whites.[95]

Jacob, a young African-American man, was arrested for drug-related offenses. While represented by a public defender, he was sentenced to four years in prison. Later, he managed to pay an attorney several thousand dollars to have the judge reconsider the sentence. It was reduced to one year followed by a court-ordered drug treatment program. Financial resources clearly make a huge difference in the outcome of drug offenses in the criminal justice system.

There's another troubling statistic. In 2017, more than 20 million Americans sought treatment for a substance abuse problem. Only 12% of them actually received treatment. That's a huge improvement over prior years. In 2014, for example, only 7.5% of those seeking treatment actually received it.[96] But still: out of every eight people who

---

[94] Bose, "Results from the 2017 National Survey on Drug Use and Health: Detailed Tables, 2018
(https://www.samhsa.gov/data/sites/default/files/cbhsq-reports/NSDUHDetailedTabs2017/NSDUHDetailedTabs2017.pdf, accessed May 15, 2020).
[95] NAACP, "Criminal Justice Fact Sheet"
(https://www.naacp.org/criminal-justice-fact-sheet/, accessed May 15, 2020). Numbers for Hispanics were not included. Also see Alana Rosenburg, *et. al.*, "Comparing Black and White Drug Offenders: Implications for Racial Disparities in Criminal Justice and Reentry Policy and Programming," *J Drug Issues* 2017 47(1), 132-142
(https://www.ncbi.nlm.nih.gov/pmc/articles/PMC5614457/, accessed May 15, 2020): Blacks are more likely to be incarcerated for smaller offenses; 49% of Blacks and only 10% of whites in the study were convicted of marijuana possession compared with 7% of Blacks and 50% of whites convicted for heroin possession.
[96] Rachel N. Lipari and Struther L. Van Horn, "Trends in Substance Abuse Disorders among Adults Aged 18 or Older," *The CBHSQ Report*, SAMHSA,

seek treatment, seven *do not* receive it. The most common reason cited, by almost half of those who could not obtain treatment, was lack of insurance coverage.[97] They couldn't afford the cost.

*   *   *   *

Not all treatment methods are the same. In fact, the *goals* of different treatment methods vary. Some seek through various methods to bring the substance abuser to abstinence from substances. Others attempt to address the *abuse* of substances, returning the abuser to occasional or social use. Still others simply address the *symptoms* of addiction, such as job loss and incarceration. This creates difficulties in comparing the success rates of various types of treatment, because they don't all define recovery in the same way. If a person achieves only occasional substance use, this might be considered a success in some models and a failure in others.

One reason for this may be the confusing definitions used in the medical field. The current edition of the *Diagnostic and Statistical Manual for Mental Disorders* (DSM-V) doesn't list addiction as a condition. Instead, it uses the rather nebulous term "Substance Use Disorder." This is evaluated on criteria from four categories of characteristics:

Jun 29 2017

(https://www.samhsa.gov/data/sites/default/files/report_2790/ShortReport-2790.html, accessed August 15, 2019). Compare Rachel N. Lipari, Eunice Park-Lee, and Struther Van Horn, "America's Need For and Receipt Of Substance Abuse Treatment in 2015," *The CBHSQ Report*, SAMHSA, Sep 16 2016

(https://www.samhsa.gov/data/sites/default/files/report_2716/ShortReport-2716.html, accessed August 15, 2019) reports that 10.6% of those who sought treatment received it in 2015. The percentage receiving treatment has

[97] Bose, Table 5.50A, shows 421 of 1,033 (41%) surveyed either didn't have health insurance, or had health insurance that didn't cover treatment.

"impaired control, social impairment, risky use, [and] pharmacological indicators (tolerance and withdrawal)."[98]

This combines two different conditions identified in the previous DSM-IV, "substance use" and "dependence syndrome." Problems with substance use were most often diagnosed on the basis of hazardous using habits, while dependence focused on the physical symptoms of withdrawal and tolerance.[99] The difference is significant: Author Gabrielle Glaser, whose article in the *Atlantic* took issue with the Twelve Step approach, cites a study by the Centers for Disease Control (CDC) that found, "nine out of 10 heavy drinkers are not dependent on alcohol and, with the help of a medical professional's brief intervention, can change unhealthy habits."[100]

But neither set of criteria addresses the scientifically-recognized characteristic of addiction as compared with dependence: the continual return to substance use even after a period of separation. If anything, the new diagnosis criteria further cloud the distinction between substance users who are likely to recover without significant intervention, those who have become dependent, and those for whom addiction has become a way of life.

It should be clear that addiction, in contrast with dependence, is more than a physical problem. Yes, the addict suffers from withdrawal symptoms. There is evidence that

---

[98] "DSM Criteria for Substance Abuse Disorders," *Primary Care Addiction Toolkit: Fundamentals of Addiction*, Portico (https://www.porticonetwork.ca/web/fundamentals-addiction-toolkit/introduction/dsm-critieria, accessed August 18, 2019).

[99] Marc Shuckit and Briget F. Grant, "DSM-5 Criteria for Substance Use Disorders: Recommendations and Rationale," *Am J Psychiatry* 2013; 170:834–851 (https://ajp.psychiatryonline.org/doi/pdf/10.1176/appi.ajp.2013.120607 82, accessed August 18, 2019).

[100] Gabrielle Glaser, "The Irrationality of Alcoholics Anonymous," *Atlantic* Feb 2015 (https://www.theatlantic.com/magazine/archive/2015/04/the-irrationality-of-alcoholics-anonymous/386255/, accessed August 15, 2019).

even marijuana, if taken in sufficient quantities, can be physically addictive.[101]

When I met Jake, for example, he was in his sixth week of physical withdrawal from marijuana. He lived in a state where pot was legal, and he'd been consuming daily amounts that far exceeded the recommended medical dosage. Such cases appear rare, but they do happen. Many other drugs, including alcohol, cocaine, and opioids, *are* physically addictive.

What distinguishes addiction from dependence is that the addict returns to using repeatedly, even after the physical symptoms of withdrawal have been overcome. There is something in addiction beyond the physical craving. There is a psychological need for the drug. But the psychological need is driven by a deeper, transcendent need that could be described as spiritual.

Not everyone who becomes physically dependent on drugs is an addict. Allen and Grace, for example, were a young couple who smoked a lot of pot. Over time, they began exploring other drugs. Both became heavy, daily cocaine users. They experienced withdrawals when they didn't use.

One day, Allen decided he'd had enough. He left Grace, moved out of their home, and stopped using cocaine. I talked to him three years later, and he would have an occasional drink or smoke some pot with friends, but had never returned to using hard drugs. His story is unusual.

Grace took the more conventional path. Her addiction destroyed her life. The last time I spoke with her, she was living in her car and spending any money she received on crack cocaine.

---

[101] "Is Marijuana Addictive," National Institute on Drug Abuse, July 2019 (https://www.drugabuse.gov/publications/research-reports/marijuana/marijuana-addictive, accessed September 8, 2019) notes the possibility of addiction, but fails to adequately distinguish between addiction and "marijuana use disorder," which they claim affects up to 30% of marijuana users.

This leads to an inevitable challenge in treatment approaches. If a person engaging in occasional risky substance abuse is diagnosed with the same condition as one whose life is consumed by addiction, how can different treatment options be recommended on the basis of the diagnosis? In some ways, this is like suggesting a diagnosis of "pain," which may be caused by a hangnail or a heart attack. While it may be true, it has limited usefulness in terms of suggesting treatment options.

This has even greater implications for the *goals* of treatment. For a casual, risky user, it may be reasonable to expect moderation in behavior as a goal, and the goal of complete abstinence may be excessive. But this goal of moderated use, applied to someone who has passed into the realm of addiction in which the substance becomes the purpose and meaning of life, is unrealistic and potentially fatal.

Glaser notes this difference in her article in the *Atlantic*, "The Irrationality of Alcoholics Anonymous." She calls the program's emphasis on God and its insistence on abstinence "unscientific." For heavy drinkers or occasional abusers who are not dependent, setting the goal at complete abstinence may even be counterproductive.[102]

This may be true for people like Allen, who gave up cocaine and changed his life. He was able to return to social drinking and occasional pot use without much difficulty.

Pat, now a minister, says he used to get drunk every day. But after a powerful experience of God, he stopped. He is now able to have an occasional glass of wine without craving more.

But most addicts and alcoholics, those people for whom the drug became the center of their lives, cannot return to occasional drinking or using.

---

[102] Glaser, see for example her anecdote about "J.G."

Ben, who died with many years of sobriety, used to say, "The first time I drank, it tasted like more." There is something in us that prevents the normal functioning of logic and limitation.

For people addicted to opiates, substitution therapy is a common form of treatment endorsed by the federal government agency SAMHSA. This approach replaces heroin, a short-acting opiate, with methadone, a long-acting opiate that, while it reduces craving and can be dispensed legally, has a much longer withdrawal period.[103] It quite literally trades one addiction for another. This will be explored further in the next chapter.

Treatment facilities use vastly different approaches. They may or may not emphasize the Twelve Steps. They may or may not emphasize abstinence, behavioral changes, and psychological healing. They may or may not employ people with personal experience in recovering from addiction who can offer hope to those who are hopeless. If we consider prison as a method of "treatment" for addiction, there may not be any emphasis on recovery at all!

Many treatment approaches are likely to use some form of Cognitive Behavioral Therapy (CBT), which can address certain thinking patterns and, to an extent, provide habituation into new ways of living. However, one aspect of

---

[103] See for example Cathie E. Alderks, "Trends In The Use Of Methadone, Buprenorphine, And Extended-Release Naltrexone at Substance Abuse Treatment Facilities: 2003-2015 (Update)," *The CBHSQ Report* Aug 22 2017 (https://www.samhsa.gov/data/sites/default/files/report_3192/ShortRep ort-3192.html, accessed August 14, 2019). See also "Chapter 4: Withdrawal Management," *Clinical Guidelines for Withdrawal Management and Treatment of Drug Dependence in Closed Settings* (Geneva: World Health Organization, 2009), Sec 4.3, which compares the 4-10 day withdrawal of heroin and other common opioids to a 10-20 day withdrawal for methadone. But see for example "Going Through Methadone Withdrawal," Healthline (https://www.healthline.com/health/going-through-methadone-withdrawal#takeaway, accessed August 14, 2019), which reports that methadone withdrawal can last up to six months.

habituation is an interior desire to change *to* a new pattern. Simply changing behaviors to gain temporary relief or to avoid punishment does not change the interior *character* of the person. They must come to understand the benefit of the new behavior for its own sake, and for the internal "goods" that only the new behavior can offer.[104] In other words, it is not enough to want to escape addiction. There must be some compelling draw to the new way of life as well. As we have seen in the previous chapters, simply returning to the ways of world is an insufficient motivation for many addicts to recover.

Various other activities that are offered in support of recovery include one-on-one therapy, Dialectical Behavioral Therapy (DBT), mindfulness meditation, yoga and light exercise, non-traditional therapies such as equine therapy, and even survival training and challenges. Coexisting mental illnesses may be treated with medication and psychotherapy. Vocational and life skills may or may not be included.

*　　　　*　　　　*　　　　*

Approaches may include spiritual or religious practices. These may occur in conjunction with the Twelve Steps and/or psychological approaches, or without such approaches.

But some religious denominations are suspicious of the Twelve Steps because they believe that reliance on working the Steps equates to seeking salvation through works rather than grace. Theologian and 16th century reformer Martin Luther, whose influence continues to impact American Protestant traditions, did not believe that any human practice could improve our sinfulness. Rather, any change

---

[104] Jennifer A. Herdt, *Putting On Virtue: The Legacy of the Splendid Vices*: Chicago: University of Chicago Press, 2008, 27-30, describing Aristotle's understanding of the motivation behind habituation.

had to originate with God, not human effort. As Jennifer Herdt summarizes, "Works of the soul are no better than works of the body, for we should not be working at all."[105]

It should be noted here that the Twelve Step programs, which refer to themselves as "spiritual, not religious," do not discount the grace of God. Rather, they might say, grace is required at every step of successful recovery, and every person in recovery is a miracle.[106]

Other religious objections to the Twelve Steps include the Anonymous programs' failure to choose a specific religious approach. This was an intentional decision by Alcoholics Anonymous when it was founded. It chose to focus on the addiction to alcohol and helping people recover from it, letting its members decide later what their conception of God ought to look like. Many become Christian, but by no means all, nor is it a requirement. Religious affiliation, or lack thereof, is an entirely personal decision.

On the other hand, publicly-funded treatment facilities are generally prevented by law from using spiritual or religious approaches because of the modern interpretation of separation of church and state. The topic of God is not permitted, lest public funds be used for evangelism. Thus, many facilities that receive public funds do not mention the Twelve Steps. They may or may not (depending on local laws and interpretations) allow meetings in the facility. They may encourage members to attend Twelve Step meetings outside the facility, or they may simply *allow* them to attend. But there is often no direct guidance on how or why the Steps promote recovery.

Rodney, for example, attended a treatment program that advertised itself as based in the Twelve Steps. His exposure to the Steps consisted of a half-hour meeting in which the

---

[105] Herdt, 174-175.

[106] See, for example, *Twelve Steps and Twelve Traditions* (New York: Alcoholics Anonymous World Services, 1952), 97-98.

first three of the Steps were explained briefly, and he received a handout with a brief description of these Steps (which he never read). Attending meetings outside the facility was optional, and not encouraged. Instead, the majority of the program focused on acknowledging the negative impacts of drug use, and simple behavioral changes like calling other people in recovery and recognizing "triggering" emotional situations.

Perhaps it wasn't surprising that Rodney noticed most of the people in the program had been there before.

As this brief description of the variety of approaches shows, the practice of recovery takes many forms and embraces different theories of what addiction is. They also have very different recovery rates. A friend who worked at a government-funded facility lamented that fewer than 10% of their clients remained clean and sober for even a year. In contrast, studies have shown that Twelve Step programs are about 70% effective for those who actively participate regularly over a period of months.[107] A two-year religious-based program that includes healing, therapy, and life skills training, claims more than 80% of those who complete the program are still clean and sober at five years.[108]

What successful approaches most often have in common is a focus on adopting a new way of life that considers the whole person, including their physical, psychological, and spiritual health. Addiction is a complex phenomenon, and holistic approaches are more likely to be effective.

---

[107] Lee Ann Kaskutas, "Alcoholics Anonymous Effectiveness: Faith Meets Science," *J Addict Dis.* 2009; 28(2): 145–157.
doi: 10.1080/10550880902772464
(https://www.ncbi.nlm.nih.gov/pmc/articles/PMC2746426/, accessed August 14, 2019).
[108] Washington.

One of the only treatment approaches that actually includes medical treatment beyond short-term attention to withdrawal symptoms is substitution therapy, also called methadone maintenance or medication-assisted treatment (MAT). While methadone remains a popular substitute for heroin, a combination of drugs called Suboxone has exceeded methadone in use, achieving more than a billion dollars in annual sales and, according to its manufacturer, holding 57% of the market share.[109]

Substitution therapy uses a long-acting opioid to maintain a stable presence in the body, reducing cravings for short-acting opioids like heroin, Fentanyl, and Oxycontin. An article on the National Institute of Health's website describes the treatment goals of substitution therapy as,

> to relieve the patient's narcotic craving, suppress the abstinence syndrome, and block the euphoric effects associated with heroin. The overall goal is to improve the patient's health and quality of life. Intermediate objectives include improving patients' access to and utilization of health care, teaching them to reduce their risk for infectious diseases such as HIV and

---

[109] "Full Year 2017 Adjusted Financial Results In-Line with Guidance," *Indivior*, February 15, 2018 (http://www.indivior.com/wp-content/uploads/2018/02/Indivior-PLC-FY-2017-Financial-Results.pdf, accessed August 22, 2019).

hepatitis, and helping them build healthy relationships and reenter the workforce or school.[110]

One treatment website calls this "harm reduction." It explains, "The idea behind harm reduction is not to necessarily eliminate substance abuse but to diminish its harmful effects."[111] The goal of this therapy, then, is not to get people off drugs, and not to give them a new purpose for living. It is intended simply to mitigate the symptoms and behavior associated with their drug use.

One obvious objective is to relieve the burden of addiction on public services, including health care and the prison system, though whether this is a driving factor in these therapies is not clear.

The actual experience of addicts who have tried substitution therapy is often radically different from the descriptions of its promoters. In my own story, above, I mentioned a friend who was in his fourth month of methadone withdrawal, who convinced me to try a meeting instead of methadone. With his permission, here is more of his story.

Ed is a musician who was addicted to heroin for years. In an effort to avoid heroin withdrawal, he tried methadone. This treated the withdrawal symptoms and reduced his cravings for heroin, for a while.

"The main difference," he says, "is that the replacements (methadone and Suboxone) are longer lasting and more stable, so your tolerance doesn't go up. You don't need more to just feel 'normal' like you would with other opiates."

---

[110] Ira J. Marion, "Methadone Treatment at Forty," *Sci Pract Perspect* 2005 Dec; 3(1): 25–31
(https://www.ncbi.nlm.nih.gov/pmc/articles/PMC2851029/, accessed August 18, 2019).
[111] "Harm Reduction Guide," American Addiction Centers, July 19, 2019 (https://americanaddictioncenters.org/harm-reduction, accessed August 22, 2019).

But he still craved heroin. "For me, methadone was my morning wake-up," he explains. "I'd go to the methadone clinic and then go to work, and then get some heroin at the end of the day. The methadone just kept me from getting dope-sick [i.e. experiencing withdrawal symptoms]."

Methadone, an "opioid agonist' that activates the opioid receptors in the brain, is supposed to prevent not only withdrawals, but also the benefit of doing heroin.[112] But Ed tells me, "I felt heroin, and I'd feel withdrawals if I didn't do it at the end of the day. Me and all the guys from the methadone clinic would get together and shoot dope all the time. Methadone isn't anything that blocks it altogether."

Unsurprisingly, this life of methadone *and* heroin became even more miserable than what he'd had before. "Methadone is just really a replacement," he says. "It doesn't address the issue. It's really a postponement. But it's easier to get off the opiates than it is to get off the replacements."

Official documentation says that heroin withdrawal lasts 5-10 days, and methadone withdrawal lasts 10-20 days.[113] But, unlike heroin, methadone is fat soluble. It can stay in the body much longer than short acting opioids. Ed was in his fourth month of methadone withdrawal when he counseled me against it.

---

[112] "An agonist is a drug that activates certain receptors in the brain. Full agonist opioids activate the opioid receptors in the brain fully resulting in the full opioid effect. Examples of full agonists are heroin, oxycodone, methadone, hydrocodone, morphine, opium and others. Partial agonist opioids activate the opioid receptors in the brain, but to a much lesser degree than a full agonist. Buprenorphine is an example of a partial agonist." UDHS, "Pharmacological Treatment" (https://www.ihs.gov/opioids/recovery/pharmatreatment/, accessed May 15, 2020).

[113] "Clinical Guidelines for Withdrawal Management and Treatment of Drug Dependence in Closed Settings," WHO, 2019, 4.2 (**https://www.ncbi.nlm.nih.gov/books/NBK310652/**, accessed September 11, 2019).

He tells me now, "I felt like crap for six months, and wasn't really right for a year. During that time, I needed to stay in constant contact with other addicts and other alcoholics in order for me to have perspective on my recovery."

Methadone isn't like other common street drugs. The withdrawal goes on and on, and it's easy to feel different, even hopeless.

Ed says, "You *can* get off of it, but you need a lot of support. It was always great when I found another methadonian, which is what we called each other. It's kind of like when you find someone who has experienced a trauma that you can relate to."

Methadone, rather than treating Ed's addiction, ultimately made it worse. He ended up, like so many others, finding recovery in a Twelve Step program. He's now been clean and sober more than twenty-five years.

Ed's estranged wife, the mother of his children, wasn't so lucky. The combination of long-term methadone use and other street drugs caused respiratory problems, kidney failure, and other major health problems. Three years ago, she went into a coma and died.[114]

Ed's story is not unique, but neither is it universal. Substitution therapy remains controversial among both addicts and medical experts. Jennifer Matesa, a recovering addict who writes extensively on addiction, notes the pros and cons of substitution therapy on her blog, "Guinevere Gets Sober."[115] She notes that industry marketing continues to tout Suboxone as non-addictive, while some doctors recommend substitution for short periods only—for detox,

---

[114] Ed Marshall, telephone interview, August 21, 2019. Used with permission.

[115] Jennifer Matesa, "Is It Easy to Quit Suboxine?" Guinevere Gets Sober, April 22, 2019 (http://guineveregetssober.com/how-hard-is-it-to-quit-suboxone/#more-4397, accessed August 22, 2019).

not for maintenance. Others see substitution as a better option than abstinence, simply because the rate of long-term success in medical treatment for people addicted to opiates is close to zero.

Substitution therapy is, at least in theory, effective as long as the substitution lasts, though Ed's story casts doubt even on that.

Matesa emphasizes that substitution therapy is best used as a method of getting off opioids altogether, but should be combined with other support systems like the Twelve Steps, and used under trained medical supervision. Unfortunately, she notes, there has been little scientific study of opioid addiction. And many professionals who provide treatment don't have sufficient knowledge or training.

As Ed says, "It's like your gardener doing Lasix surgery. He can read a book on it and know all the terminology, but do you really want him working on your eyes?"

This discussion also highlights the different standards of success between recovery approaches. The addiction substitution approach does not consider being chemical-free a characteristic of recovery. Some other approaches consider social drinking to be acceptable. Some measure abstinence at five years, or one, or at the end of the ninety-day program.

The Twelve Step groups have not measured their own success rates, and since they are anonymous they have been difficult for scholars to study. Formal studies are now showing what Twelve Step participants have long accepted as true: The Steps have remarkable rates of long-term recovery for those who are willing to work them.

CHAPTER FOURTEEN
SEEKING SUCCESSFUL RECOVERY

As mentioned in Chapter Twelve, nearly 90% of those who seek treatment don't get it, often because they can't afford it. But not all forms of treatment cost a lot. Twelve Step programs cost nothing, and many church-based programs are low-cost or tailored to your ability to pay.[116] Why, then, do people fail to find recovery in these low- and no-cost programs?

One major factor is managing withdrawal symptoms. Withdrawal from alcohol, for example, can be fatal without medical attention. So can withdrawal from some tranquilizers. Withdrawal from benzodiazepines, such as Valium and Xanax, can last for months and cause major psychotic reactions.[117]

But no withdrawal is pleasant. Jim went to the hospital emergency room for help with his heroin detox. The doctor, who happened to be in recovery himself, told him, "Heroin withdrawal won't kill you. It just feels like it will." Even when

---

[116] For example, Bridge Ministry in Buckingham, VA, a residential program, asks for a $600 processing fee and $200 per week—and waives these fees for participants who can't pay. "Apply," Bridge Ministry (http://www.bridgeministry.info/apply-.html, accessed August 15, 2019).

[117] "Alcohol Withdrawal," Harvard Health Publishing April 2019 (https://www.health.harvard.edu/a_to_z/alcohol-withdrawal-a-to-z, accessed August 14, 2019); "Drug and Alcohol Withdrawal," Addictions and Recovery Apr 12 2019 (https://www.addictionsandrecovery.org/withdrawal.htm, accessed August 14, 2019); H. Pétursson, "The Benzodiazepine Withdrawal Syndrome," *Addiction* 1994 Nov; 89(11):1455-9 (https://www.ncbi.nlm.nih.gov/pubmed/7841856, accessed August 14, 2019).

doctor-supervised withdrawal is not medically necessary, the misery of withdrawal is one of the major hurdles discouraging addicts from quitting drugs.

Some may have tried spiritual or faith-based programs and found them wanting. Researchers Ellen Meara and Richard G. Frank note that not every form of treatment is effective for every person suffering from addiction.

> The potential benefits of treatment vary across individuals for many reasons. Some individuals may not benefit from treatments due to an especially severe addiction, or co-occurring mental disorders that render common treatment ineffective. At the other extreme, recent evidence on alcohol dependence suggests that a substantial number of individuals with substance use disorders will recover without treatment.[118]

Some, including Gabrielle Glaser, argue that the "one size fits all" approach of the Twelve Step groups is outdated because it fails those who are not actually addicted.[119] Certainly the approach was not designed for those with an occasional problem, but rather for those whose life is consumed by their substance of choice.

Even if this criticism is appropriate, it is misplaced. As noted previously AA, for example, has from its inception made the distinction between the "heavy drinker" and the "real alcoholic." This distinction has been blurred not by AA,

---

[118] Ellen Meara and Richard G. Frank, "Spending on Substance Abuse Treatment: How Much is Enough?" Addiction. 2005 Sep; 100(9): 1240–1248. Doi: 10.1111/j.1360-0443.2005.01227.x
(https://www.ncbi.nlm.nih.gov/pmc/articles/PMC1402649/, accessed August 14, 2019). Note that this finding may suggest that the difference between dependence and addiction has not been adequately distinguished within the larger category of Substance Use Disorders.
[119] Glaser.

but by the medical community which, until recently, had no effective treatments to offer *other than* the Twelve Step programs—and which, as changes to DSM-V indicate, increasingly makes little distinction in *degree* of substance abuse.

Several criticisms of the Twelve Step model are currently fashionable. One is that it has, overall, low rates of recovery. Glaser, for example, cites a report claiming AA's success rate is "between 5 and 8 percent." I don't doubt that those statistics are fairly accurate with respect to everyone who attends a meeting. But the vast majority of those who attend Twelve Step meetings do not actually get involved in working the program. Despite the emphasis placed on the actual work of change (the Steps), many who attend meetings incorrectly perceive the meetings themselves to be the mechanism of recovery.

Among those who do get involved, recovery rates are far better. Studies of Twelve Step participation among veterans coming out of inpatient treatment facilities show that Twelve Step participants are twice as likely to be abstinent at one year and at 18 months if they attend meetings (40-50% compared with 20-25% of those who did not attend), and that the success rate in Twelve Step participation improves with the number of meetings participants attend. A study of participants who attended meetings at least weekly found that 70% were still sober at two years. Of those who attended regularly for more than six months, 70% were still sober at the 16-year follow-up![120] Not surprisingly, these studies confirm that regular participation provides better results.

Gabrielle Glaser and others claim that the Twelve Step programs blame the victim by suggesting that if the addict doesn't recover, it's the fault of the addict for not doing

---

[120] Kaskutas.

enough.[121] Twelve Step programs are voluntary and lack an imposed structure. Yes, newcomers are told to go to meetings, get a sponsor, and work the Steps. But there is no authority to force them to take these actions, no house manager or drug testing to ensure abstinence, and no attendance check at meetings. It's very easy to attend a meeting or two, *not* get involved, and never understand how the Steps work.

Many, many people fall into this trap. There seems to be no practical way to measure whether, or how diligently, a participant actually works the Steps.

For example, I met Chad in a meeting where he identified as being new. It was his first meeting, and I explained to him that he should find a sponsor to guide him through the process of working the Steps. I offered to be that guide if he wanted me to. I saw him a second time, but he avoided talking to me. I never saw him again after that. Did the Twelve Step program fail him? Or did he fail to use it as directed?

Adrian attended meetings for over a year. He got a sponsor, but rarely called him. He didn't work the Steps. He was convinced that meetings alone would keep him sober.

Adrian's fall seemed to begin when he used mouthwash before the meeting in an apparent effort to be more attractive to women. After swishing, he would swallow the mouthwash, which contained a significant amount of alcohol. Within two months, he was drunk again. He stopped going to meetings soon afterward, and I never saw him after that.

---

[121] For example, Lance Dodes and Zachary Dodes, "The Psuedoscience of Alcoholics Anonymous: There's a Better Way to Treat Addiction," *Salon* Mar 23, 2014
(https://www.salon.com/2014/03/23/the_pseudo_science_of_alcoholics_anonymous_theres_a_better_way_to_treat_addiction/, accessed August 15, 2019), though this article badly mischaracterizes Twelve Step programs and even claims that the Twelve Step approach receives government financial support.

On the other hand, I met Robert at a meeting when he was coming off a binge and seemed desperate. He asked for my phone number, and I gave it to him. I never saw him again after that. The program had apparently failed him.

But early one morning, I got a phone call from Robert. He'd come out of a blackout in a cheap hotel room in another city, and had no idea how he got there.

"You've got to help me," he pleaded. "I get it now."

I helped him find a meeting and a ride to it, and he gratefully went.

By many standards, including scientific standards, Robert would have been considered a failure because he tried to stay clean and did not do so. Just because a person doesn't succeed the first time, and may not even be convinced that they are truly an addict, doesn't mean they can't recover given the right set of circumstances.

*　　　*　　　*　　　*

People who are truly addicted most often are motivated by *desperation* and *hope*. The specific circumstances that motivate them can't be predicted. In my own history, I can point to many events that seemingly should have provided such motivation: being fired from my job, getting beat up while trying to buy drugs, and getting arrested for DUI, for example. It was my inability to pay rent that precipitated my eventual recovery. It wasn't the first time it had happened. But, for some mysterious reason, this time was different. It caused what the Twelve Step programs call "a moment of clarity." I became willing to ask for help.

But it wasn't the first time I had asked for help, either. My health insurer had referred me to a counseling center that supposedly specialized in substance abuse issues. My intake interview went something like this:

Interviewer: "What brings you here today?"

Me: "I have a problem with cocaine, and my life is a mess."

Interviewer: "You sound depressed. Do you think you're depressed?"

Me: "Yes. I can't stop using cocaine."

Interviewer: "Well, I'm very concerned about this depression. Let's talk about how we can help you with that."

At first, this gave me hope. Here was a medical professional telling me that I used cocaine because I was depressed. Clearly, if I could stop being depressed, then I'd be able to stop using cocaine.

At the facility's recommendation, I attended a group therapy session for depression. But none of the other participants ever mentioned having a problem with substances. They had more classic depression symptoms. I, on the other hand, was depressed about not having any money and being miserable all the time. Cocaine was the *cause* of these, not the symptom.

The experience further reinforced my belief that no one could understand me, and that I was beyond hope.

Several years later, the possibility of a Twelve Step program was suggested to me not by a medical professional, but by another addict. I knew him, and I knew he used like I did. He said the Twelve Steps were working for him. I remained skeptical, of course, but I became willing to see what they were all about.

Twelve Step programs are amazingly effective for those who actively participate in them. Some critics have referred to the Steps as an antibiotic that doesn't work but we blame the patient. Before making such a claim, a scientific approach would first verify that the patient was actually taking the antibiotic as directed. If not, it might address the question of *why not*.

Getting clean and sober in a Twelve Step program takes desperation. It's been said that these programs are for people who have exhausted all other possibilities. They are the "last stop," the "end of the line." That was once true, though their success has led many in the medical and criminal justice fields to steer people to Twelve Step programs long before they have reached "the end of the line."

It may be equally true that there are people who cannot get clean and sober without an imposed structure, no matter how desperate they may be. I've seen people fail to recover despite a seemingly overwhelming desire to quit,

Francis was one of these. He'd been drinking and using since he was a teenager, and now faced a felony DUI charge. But, no matter what I tried with him, he couldn't stay clean and sober for more than a few days.

After months, of trying, he disappeared. One of my friends later saw him at a state mental hospital, where he'd been hospitalized indefinitely for "wet brain," a generally-irreversible form of brain damage caused by alcohol abuse.

Jim, who struggled with heroin withdrawal for two years and eventually died in the park, was another.

Why do these people, who so desperately desire recovery, not attain it? I have never heard a satisfactory answer.

Working a Twelve Step program takes self-discipline, something addicts are not known for having. This is also true of habituation, cognitive behavioral therapy, or any other approach to changing our thinking.

Perhaps that's why pharmaceutical solutions have become increasingly popular. You don't have to do any work, just take a pill. It's easy to see why this approach might appeal to professionals, who have seen so many addicts fail to recover, as well as to people whose loved ones struggle. But if a person switches their addiction from heroin to methadone, for example, have they really solved the problem?

*   *   *   *

Some people who do not suffer from the compulsion of addiction may at some point be able to return to social substance use. It is tempting to ask *why* one would want to return to behavior that has been problematic in the past, and whether that is in fact rational behavior. But for those who can do so without danger, that is a less important question.

For most addicts, though, abstinence is critical to recovery. We can't be fooled by the hope we may some day be able to drink or use socially.

There are several reasons for this. The first is that, as addicts, we tend to have a subconscious obsession to return to successfully to using our drug of choice. Our minds will occasionally try to convince us that this is actually a good idea. And sometimes, if we are in a stressful or weakened emotional state, we may become convinced.[122] Any of us will have ample evidence that there's no such thing as one helping of our drug of choice.

Second, even other drugs are dangerous for us. Alcohol and marijuana, whether or not they were among our substances of choice, can compromise our logical thinking. They lower our inhibitions. Things that would not sound like a good idea sober suddenly *do* sound like good ideas.

Nikki, for example, had finally gotten five years off of heroin after decades of addiction and literally dozens of treatment centers. One day, at a social function, she decided it would be okay to have a glass of red wine. That worked so well, she began having a glass or two of wine every day. Then

---

[122] *Alcoholics Anonymous* (43) writes, "The alcoholic at certain times has no effective mental defense against the first drink."

smoking a joint seemed like a social thing to do. It was legal in that state, after all.

Within six months, she was back on heroin. She lost her marriage and her family, and almost died.

Charlie came into a Twelve Step program after falling down the stairs while drunk in his college dorm where he drank every day. He worked the Steps and stayed sober for five years. One day he decided he could have one drink. Afterward, ashamed, he immediately came back to the program. He stayed sober another five years.

Then his brain got the better of him. He decided that he'd celebrate this milestone with one drink, as he had before. But this time, one drink turned into a months-long binge. Charlie couldn't stop drinking.

I happened to call Charlie about a work matter one day, and asked him how he was doing.

"Not well," he said. "I can't stop drinking. Could we meet for coffee tomorrow?"

Of course I agreed.

But that night, Charlie lost control of his car while drunk and hit a telephone pole. He was killed instantly.

After Charlie's first experience of having one drink, it might be reasonable to assume he could return to social drinking. But his second attempt was quite different: It led to his death. This stands as a stark warning not to generalize the view that a substance abuser can return to social use.

Charlie's story illustrates another principle that should not be overlooked: when an addict finally does seek help, time is of the essence. Delay can be fatal.

The third reason for considering abstinence essential is this: A spiritual approach requires a clear head and all our faculties. Yes, sometimes people on drugs pray and meditate. They often think they are fully present. Adam thought so when he decided, under the influence of LSD, to meditate outside in a snowstorm in his boxer shorts. He lost three toes.

Drugs affect how our brain works. That's their purpose. Others have told me, and I have I have found through my own experience, that *any* mind-altering drug reduces my awareness of spiritual realities. In my own belief system, I would put it this way: Drugs separate me from God, and without God I can't stay in recovery.

For all these reasons, recovery from addiction *for those who are addicted* must include abstinence.

*   *   *   *

As we consider various approaches to treatment, we will note that they tend to focus on different *aspects* of addiction. Recalling those developed at the beginning of this book, we might expect that an approach to recovery would be most successful if it provided the elements we identified as necessary for recovery from addiction:

- Hope (successful examples of recovery)
- Support for successful separation from drugs (and a stated goal of abstinence)
- Direction for daily living
- Purpose and meaning for life beyond our own selfish ends
- Repairing what separates us from the world
- Healing the underlying trauma and associated wounds

It should not be surprising, then, that the more comprehensive an approach and the more it focuses on purpose and meaning for life, the more effective that approach would be. One can see that religious and spiritual aspects have an advantage *if they are combined* with other healing and practical aspects.

Addiction is a condition that affects the whole person: physical, mental, and spiritual. But some approaches favor one area at the expense of the others. Some in the scientific community are dismissive of spirituality, and some in the religious community are equally suspicious of science.

Recovery, if it is to be successful, must address the whole person. Here we might make a distinction between *abstinence*, simply refraining from drinking or using, and *sobriety* or *recovery*, a way of life that allows us to live without the *desire* to drink and use. The difference is important. Abstinence is simply resisting temptation, an approach that is unsustainable for most addicts. Recovery means *removing* the temptation, which promotes long-term success.

Chapter Fifteen
When Recovery Fails

What does it mean when recovery fails? Is it the failure of the addict, or the failure of the program? These are not easy questions to answer, particularly because there is little agreement as to what constitutes success or failure in recovery.

Some experts, for example, consider a medical view of success. If a person has a disease, such as cancer, a treatment may be *temporarily* successful. In other words, it may reduce the cancer or prevent it from worsening. If the cancer later returns or accelerates, this is a worsening of the *condition*, not a failure of the treatment.

This approach could be generalized to absurd conclusions. For example, if a person has an infection, and a new antibiotic merely prevents it from getting worse but fails to cure it, is that antibiotic a success or not? Most people would say that, if other antibiotics would eliminate the infection entirely, the antibiotic that merely prevents it from worsening does not measure up.

How these medical measures of success apply to addiction is not at all clear. Take Ed, for example, the man who convinced me to go to my first Twelve Step meeting. Up to that point, he'd tried treatment programs and methadone. Neither had made a difference. When he took me to my first meeting, the Twelve Steps had helped him to stop drinking entirely for several months, and to cut his heroin use back to merely occasional. By some standards, that would be considered a huge success. In the Twelve Step programs, it's not.

Ed's limited success was temporary. Over the next few weeks, he went back to using regularly. He lost his home and his family. He did some time in jail.

It took ten years for Ed to come back to the program. This time, he got completely clean and stayed that way. He's been clean and sober for 25 years without a relapse. Today, Ed runs a successful business and is known for his quality work. He also continues to work with other addicts seeking recovery.

At what point does one evaluate Ed's success in recovery? By most measures, apart from a few weeks of mitigation, he failed completely for nearly two decades. Yet there came a point at which the Twelve Steps provided something they had not provided in the past. He got clean and sober, and has stayed that way.

*   *   *   *

Such stories are not uncommon. Ebby, the man who "carried the message" to Alcoholics Anonymous co-founder Bill W., continued to relapse for most of his life. In 1934, during a period of sobriety, Ebby introduced Bill to what would become the Twelve Steps. But Ebby did not achieve long-term sobriety until 1964, two years before his death.[123]

On the other hand, I once met a woman who got clean and sober at the age of twelve. She'd been a street kid, breaking into houses and stealing drugs and alcohol. When I met her, she'd been clean fifteen years and was just finishing grad school.

---

[123] Will Waldron, "These Exalted Acres: Unlocking the Secrets of Albany Rural Cemetery," *Times Union* (Albany, NY, https://www.timesunion.com/albanyrural/ethacher/, accessed August 20, 2019).

And there are plenty of instances where someone stays clean and sober for years or even decades, but later decides to try the experiment of one drink or drug, with predictable results.

The standard of the Twelve Step program, as described in meetings, is that you're a success if you remain abstinent today. But from a practical standpoint, in which length of sobriety is honored regularly, ultimately you are a success if you die sober. Perhaps this presents a seemingly impossible standard. Who of us knows when we will die, much less how and in what condition? There is no guarantee that we will never drink or use drugs again. Yet the number of Twelve Step members with uninterrupted, long-term recovery cannot be ignored. It works for many people. I happen to be one of them.

Twelve Step recovery emphasizes work with others who suffer from addiction. As we do this, we encounter some people who recover and many who don't. The question each of us struggles with is this: Why do some addicts seem unable to recover no matter what they do or how badly they want to change?

We have no answer. So far, science and medicine have not provided a satisfactory answer either. And it's likely that there is no single answer, and no silver bullet that will work in every instance.

Studies have increasingly linked addiction with mental illness, for example. Jim, who died in the park after years of trying to get clean, had psychotic episodes when he wasn't using drugs.

Sandy found, once she stopped drinking, that she was afflicted with bipolar disorder, and regularly had manic episodes that required hospitalization. She did remain sober, but her mental illness didn't make this easy.

Gary struggles with depression that conventional psychiatric treatments have failed to relieve. He only finds relief in drugs and alcohol, and can't seem to stay clean and sober for more than a few weeks at a time.

Stan had been clean and sober a year when a schizophrenic episode led him to drink again. He lived on the street for five years before surfacing again in another city.

But mental illness can't explain every instance of failure. My friend Ed had no mental illness, but was unsuccessful in quitting for almost twenty years. When he did finally get clean, no mental illness became evident.

Jack was in and out of Twelve Step for five years, trying to get off heroin. He occasionally managed a few months off the drug, but always returned to it. He seemed hopeless. But one day, something happened and he became able to stop. He's now been clean for more than five years.

In some of these examples, the presence or absence of mental illness did not become apparent until the person achieved recovery. Often the symptoms of a mental illness cannot be differentiated from the symptoms of addiction. Paranoia, mood swings, and even hallucinations are often caused by drug or alcohol use or withdrawal. It can be difficult even for professionals to distinguish between addiction and mental illness. And psychiatric treatment for someone still drinking or using is complicated at best. Responsible psychiatrists are rightly hesitant to prescribe medications on top of the medications a patient may already be using. Some medications have serious interactions when taken with alcohol, opiates, or other drugs.[124]

---

[124] See, for example, "Does Abilify Interact with other Medications?" WebMD (https://www.webmd.com/drugs/2/drug-64439/abilify-oral/details/list-interaction-medication, accessed August 20, 2019), and Daniel K. Hall-Flavin, "Antidepressants and Alcohol: What's the Concern?" Mayo Clinic (https://www.mayoclinic.org/diseases-conditions/depression/expert-answers/antidepressants-and-alcohol/faq-20058231, accessed August 20, 2019).

On the other hand, despite the relatively primitive state of mental health care, in many instances even serious mental illness *can* be controlled in conjunction with recovery. Again, we are left with the question, "Why do some recover and others don't?"

Perhaps this can be explained by the need for motivation and hope. People naturally tend to resist change. Subconsciously, we think the misery we know is better than the unknown. And, as psychologist David Sack notes, some don't believe they deserve better. Whether because of parenting or trauma, they don't believe happiness is possible, or if it is possible that they don't deserve it. Sack notes not only the incidence of traumas, but of mental illnesses, including anxiety and depression, which he says affect as many as 20% of American adults.[125]

*   *   *   *

In the case of addiction, as with so many other life situations, there usually has to be some event that triggers the desire to seek help, something that makes our comfortable misery less comfortable.

This is what is sometimes called "hitting bottom." This doesn't mean, as is sometimes suggested, that we lose everything. There is always more to lose so long as we're alive. Where there's breath, there's hope.

"Hitting bottom" means reaching a point that is lower than we thought possible for us. This may be getting fired from a job, getting arrested, or losing one's family. It may be a health diagnosis. It may be a particularly shameful lapse of

---

[125] David Sack, "Are You Addicted to Unhappiness?" *Psychology Today* March 5, 2014 (https://www.psychologytoday.com/us/blog/where-science-meets-the-steps/201403/are-you-addicted-unhappiness, accessed August 20, 2019).

behavior. Even an intervention by friends and family can have this effect, though in my experience it's rarely sufficient.

The trouble is, what it takes to shake an addict out of their comfortable misery cannot be predicted. It depends on many things, including upbringing, history, perception of strengths, and so forth. For example, if someone prides themselves on being employed, the loss of a job may be the event that gets their attention and motivates change. If they have a history of unemployment, losing a job is less likely to be enough.

Tony, an attorney, hit bottom after getting fired for showing up at court drunk.

Ray's "bottom" was getting drunk on the east coast and waking up on a beach in California—with no money in his pocket and no idea where he was. Formerly a successful salesman, he spent weeks living at the Salvation Army and going to meetings before he could raise enough money to get home again.

Miriam's was when child protective services came to take away her youngest child—the other two had already been taken.

Cliff's came when he lost his job as a firefighter, the only thing he'd ever wanted to do.

Alex's came after he'd run up a $40,000 tab with his dealer. Unable to pay, Alex was sleeping when the dealer put several bullets through the front window of his home.

Phil's was when he came to in a strange city and realized he'd stolen money from the Mafia. His tale of making amends at the risk of his life remains one of the most powerful stories I've ever heard.

Ben's came as he lay in bed next to his wife, too high to sleep. He says he felt a hand slap him across the face, and a deep voice asked him, "What are you doing?" He never drank or used drugs again.

Yet, as emphasized in previous chapters, *motivation* alone is not enough. There must also be *hope* that some alternative life is possible. This is sometimes the more challenging of the two necessities. We've *tried* to fit into the world in the past, and it hasn't worked.

For us to have hope, something new has to be offered. At the very least, something we haven't seen before has to be presented. So, for example, someone who has tried the Twelve Step approach unsuccessfully in the past must be convinced that they've missed something, or else they'll believe it's the same old story that doesn't work for them. The same is true of church, or of any other form of treatment.

Here's an example: Pat, a struggling addict, had tried Twelve Step programs many times in the past. He never stayed clean more than a few weeks, and was convinced that they wouldn't work for him. But, while in a moment of desperation, Pat met Bill, who had been in addiction but has been clean in a Twelve Step program for several years. Bill first told Pat his story, establishing his credentials. Then he asked Pat if he'd just gone to meetings, or if he'd actually gotten a sponsor and worked the Steps. Pat had gotten a sponsor once, but had rarely called him, and had never gotten beyond Step Three. He'd never made a personal inventory, never shared his faults with another human being, and never cleaned up his past. He still didn't understand what that had to do with staying off drugs.

Bill explained that he doesn't really understand how that helps to stay off drugs, either. But Bill was told to do it, and when he did it worked. He challenged Pat to ask anyone in any meeting who says they're coming back from a relapse whether they'd been calling their sponsor and working the Steps when the relapse began. Bill knows, because his sponsor suggested this to him, that the odds of finding someone who actually *was* doing these things when they relapsed are pretty small.

This gave Pat hope. He *hadn't* actually done the program fully. He'd skipped some parts. He didn't yet realize that he'd skipped the most important parts. But his desperation was sufficient, and Pat grasped the hope Bill offered him. He tried the Twelve Step program again—this time doing the actual work of recovery. And this time, Pat stayed clean.

But here's the catch: there has to actually *be* hope in the message. The Twelve Steps offer literally millions of success stories showing that they work. There are other approaches, many of them religious, that have good track records for success. But I've heard people promise that if you just meditate daily, or if you chant these particular words, or if you believe the right thing, or of you go to therapy, you'll be able to return to the world of work and responsibility without craving drugs. I haven't seen many people succeed.

Remember, a successful replacement for the "religion" of addiction must fill the holes addiction tries to fill. It must offer an order for daily life, a purpose or meaning beyond ourselves, and some form of habituation that changes our thinking by reprogramming our behavior. The Twelve Step programs do this well. Where they tend to fall short is in the deep healing of the underlying traumas.

*　　　　*　　　　*　　　　*

There are psychological approaches that offer some of these elements. Psychology recognizes the importance of meaning in life, for example. One study cited by researchers finds "positive life meaning related to strong religious beliefs, self-transcendent values, membership in groups, dedication to a cause, and clear life goals."

But psychology, while it recognizes the importance of meaning, seems to have little to offer in actually finding that meaning.

Another study found that "religiosity may form one important source of meaning," to the degree that it provides meaning for life.[126] For example, some faith traditions have little interest in life in this world, seeing it only as a temporary phase before whatever comes next. The meaning of life would seem to be death, which is hardly a compelling answer. Others provide only fellowship with little real purpose or moral guidance. Many lack sufficient fellowship to support the recovering addict, meeting only on Sundays and having little contact in between. And few offer specific guidance for reordering one's daily life. But a religious path that provides meaning and guidance *can* be effective in helping addicts.

Offering some meaning for life, along with guidance for daily action and the support of people who have recovered, are elements of any successful approach to recovery. Recognizing this, we can guide addicts to more effective solutions.

But the real mystery is what it takes to make someone desperate enough to change. Unfortunately, some never reach that level of desperation. They may die from risky use of substances, substance-related accidents, overdose, or violence.

Others may go on to the bitter end where their body fails them without ever acknowledging that the substance is the problem. These are the baffling cases. How can they not see that their own behavior is killing them? But remember, crazy

---

[126] Yalom (1980) and Chamberlain and Zika (1988), cited in Sheryl Zika and Kerry Chamberlain, "On the relation between meaning in life and psychological wellbeing," *British Journal of Psychology* 83 (1992), 134-135. After surveying pre-existing research, however, the article returns to considering *how* meaning in life affects psychological wellbeing.

as it seems, if life has no meaning for them, they may not care.

One thing that people who care about addicts should know is that whatever triggers that sense of desperation is usually related to the consequences of our actions. Thus, shielding an addict from the consequences of his or her actions may *prevent* recovery. This is difficult, even for me. It is human nature to want to help people, by which we usually mean we want to relieve their suffering. But which suffering is greater: spending a year in jail or a life in addiction? Being homeless for a while or dying of a diseased liver?

Susan, who drank for many years even while caring for her children, says, "What happens when you coddle an alcoholic or an addict? They die."

There is no certain formula for getting a person into recovery. Desperation and hope are common features, but we don't know what causes the necessary desperation, or provides the necessary hope in each individual case. What we *do* know is that shielding an addict from the consequences of their actions removes an opportunity for that person to achieve the necessary desperation.

Chapter Sixteen
The Powerlessness Dilemma

The Twelve Steps, as originally published by Alcoholics Anonymous, begin with this controversial statement: "We admitted we were powerless over alcohol..."[127] This premise for recovery has been attacked in recent years as being unreasonable, unrealistic, and unscientific.[128]

Powerlessness and return to occasional use are closely linked. If we are powerless, then clearly we cannot control our use. Gabrielle Glaser references a scientific study showing that 22% of alcoholics were able to return to moderate drinking.[129] While that may sound like good news, it may also offer false hope. Richard Taite cautions that such folks are most likely not "dependent" drinkers.[130]

Even if about one in five alcoholics were successful, that means four out of five were not. Those are the same odds as playing Russian roulette with a five-round revolver and only one bullet missing, with potentially the same consequences.

One has to wonder *why* we're so obsessed with returning to moderate drinking. Why *isn't* abstinence acceptable? Yes, it can be awkward to decline a glass of wine, a beer, or even a joint in social situations, especially in the beginning. But I've become comfortable toasting a newly-married couple with

---

[127] *Alcoholics Anonymous*, 59.
[128] See, for example, Glaser; Dunnington 32-33, but cf. 165.
[129] Glaser. How their alcoholism was diagnosed is not stated.
[130] Richard Taite, "Can Alcoholics Ever Drink Moderately?" *Psychology Today* Apr 8 2014 (https://www.psychologytoday.com/us/blog/ending-addiction-good/201404/can-alcoholics-ever-drink-moderately, accessed May 15, 2020).

apple juice. Most people don't notice. Those who do are often problem drinkers themselves.

In one of the most inconceivable places to be clean and sober, a Grateful Dead concert, there was a Twelve Step meeting during the intermission at every show. Sometimes there were a few dozen participants. Sometimes there were hundreds. If we can stay abstinent comfortably with the support of others at a rock concert, in what situation is a drink or a drug actually socially necessary?

On the other hand, if we're powerless over alcohol or drugs, does that mean we can't quit? Clearly it does not, because many addicts recover using the Twelve Steps. But it does mean that we can't quit using our own resources. We've tried and failed many times. Control does not exist when it comes to our drug of choice, and often not for any other drug we may try.

*   *   *   *

The admission of powerlessness, for those who have a history of returning to addiction repeatedly, is essential for change to begin. The reason is simple: so long as we think we can control our intake, we'll continue to try. But we can't control our intake. We've proven that over and over again.

We need help. We need new information and new patterns of behavior. Some would say we need God's help. Certainly, as described in the chapter on purpose, we need something beyond ourselves toward which to reorient our lives. If we had these resources ourselves, we would have used them already.

But most often, the reason we don't accept help is that, at some level, we're obsessed with returning to moderate use. Kyle, a recovering alcoholic, once told me, "If I could drink like a normal person, I'd do it every frikkin' day!"

Dennis, who was in recovery at the time but later returned to addiction, said, "If they invented a pill where you only had to take one to be cured of addiction, I'd take six!"

We have an obsession so deep that we often don't even recognize it.

Pastor Rick Nichols works with addicts through his church, and did his doctoral dissertation on addiction and the Church. In his dissertation, he asks, "If one is powerless, then what is the motive to fight to be free?" He argues that viewing addiction as an incurable disease, like cancer, "can actually undermine self-confidence and the will to change because the addicted person believes they cannot and eventually should not fight who they really are." It creates a "victim mentality" that denies personal responsibility for one's current state.[131]

His question follows an extensive survey of material that describes addiction as sin—alienation from God.[132] Yet most Christians would be unlikely to argue that sin can be overcome purely through human effort. Some, following 16th century Protestant theologian Martin Luther, would argue that human effort is of no value at all.[133]

What Nichols seems most concerned about is the *identity* that a belief of powerlessness tends to create. If we believe we are addicts, powerless to change, we won't believe we can be anything else. When I asked Nichols to clarify his position, Nichols replied,

> What I was trying to convey [in the thesis] is that in constantly repeating "I am powerless," that we are

---

[131] Rick Nichols, "Dirty Discipleship: The Essential Nature of Recovery Ministry in Fulfilling the Great Commission" (unpublished doctoral thesis), Lynchburg, VA: Liberty University School of Divinity, 2017 (https://digitalcommons.liberty.edu/doctoral/1390, accessed September 6, 2019), 37.

[132] Ibid., 9-12.

[133] Herdt, 174-175.

creating an identity of powerlessness, in which we start to believe victory is not possible. Maybe a better phrase would be "I am powerless apart from Christ." I have personally known many people who abandoned the Twelve Steps because of the identity that is created through them. Unfortunately, the Twelve Steps, I believe, unintentionally creates an identity in the addiction rather than an identity in Christ. Therefore, the person in recovery constantly refers to themselves as "addict" and, thus, they never find victory. They instead, only find maintenance and reliance upon the Twelve Steps.[134]

While acknowledging respect for Nichols's religious views, one wonders whether "maintenance and reliance upon the Twelve Steps" is not a successful outcome for addiction. They provide an alternate way of life, and, from a religious perspective, several critical elements of Christian discipleship —elements that are found in most if not all major religions. Their lack of religious specificity allows the choice of the participant to choose Christ (or not).

As for the role of powerlessness in this process, in my own case, the admission of powerlessness merely confirmed what I had been trying to deny: that I could not recover without help. Nichols seems to agree with this, but uses different language. I would agree with him that "maintenance and reliance" on some other way of life, whether the Twelve Steps or formal Christian discipleship, is imperative for an addict to remain in recovery.

Powerlessness thus serves an important function in the recovery process. Research shows that this point of despair is often necessary for change to take place. We have to exhaust our own resources before asking for help. Only then do we

---

[134] Rick Nichols, personal email September 9, 2019.

The Soul of an Addict

find the necessary *desperation* to consider an offer of *hope*. This is especially true of addicts and alcoholics, who fear that their secrets would cause them to be shamed and outcast if they were known.

Sometimes there is validity to these fears. Blake sought help from his manager at work. For years afterward, he was passed over for promotions despite having been in recovery all that time. He recalls that once, at a company party where he sipped soda water, a drunk manager asked him how his drinking problem was going.

Sandra sought help from her pastor after a relapse into pills. The resulting interaction left her feeling shamed, misunderstood, unheard, and rejected.

Robert, an elementary school teacher, didn't dare ask for help even as his liver failed, fearing that the school district would fire him.

Those of us who are already in recovery are unlikely to be shocked by anything another addict might tell us. Just today, a man in a halfway house confided to me that he had relapsed two days before. If the house management learned of it, he would have been kicked out, and he had nowhere else to go. Despite my assurances of confidentiality, he remained worried that I'd stop by the manager's office before leaving and tell his secret. (I didn't. Confidentiality means confidentiality.)

*   *   *   *

Kent Dunnington argues, "[A]ddiction is an exercise of self-assertion and control that leads the addicted person to deny his own underlying disorder and disunity."[135] In other words, the addict believes he or she is in control. We cannot admit that we are not, because that would mean there is no hope.

---

[135] Dunnington, 179.

We would be admitting our failure, our utter inability to cope with life. And while this denial persists, he or we cannot acknowledge our alienation, our sin, or our55 powerlessness to change.

Sam was a good example. In a Twelve Step program, he was able to stay clean for a year. To celebrate, he took his dream vacation—alone, and without support. He got loaded. For the next two years, he was in and out of meetings, always looking for a plan to get his drug use back under control.

One day, he called me.

"I have a plan to quit using," he said. He explained how he would live in a camper in the desert, miles from the nearest town, and theoretically unable to obtain any drugs.

"What do you think?" he asked me.

I replied, "I think you have a plan to quit using. You're still trying to manage this yourself."

A few weeks later, Sam died of an overdose.

This highlights the importance of the admission of powerlessness. Our addiction is based on the self-deception that we have it under control. We blame our problems on the world, not the drug. We cannot even consider that our "god" might be false. And so long as we cling to our old god, there is no room for a new one.

Susan says, "Admitting my powerlessness was a huge relief. I always thought I was supposed to be able to fix this on my own. Once I admitted I couldn't, I could stop trying and ask for help."

Powerlessness is our admission that the false god has failed us. We have chosen the wrong purpose for our lives. Our best thinking has destroyed us.

We need help.

There's another piece: So long as we think we're in control, we can't admit the truth to anyone else, either. *They* may see our affliction, and often others see it more clearly than we do. But *we* can't admit it. At some level, we know we're failing. We have shame, self-doubt, even self-hatred. But we can't tell anyone, because that would force us to admit it to ourselves.

We are separated from other people by our secrets.

Researcher Brené Brown tells us that people need to share in order to heal.[136] We need to become vulnerable, which means truthful, and that can't happen so long as we deceive ourselves that we're in control of our addiction.

Some have observed that the powerlessness controversy is really unnecessary. AA does not claim that we *remain* powerless. The very next step, Step Two, insists, that we "Came to believe that a power greater than ourselves could restore us to sanity."[137]

Elsewhere, the book says of our addiction, "We could wish to be moral, we could wish to be philosophically comforted, in fact, we could will these things with all our might, but the needed power wasn't there. Our human resources, as marshaled [sic] by the will, were not sufficient; they failed utterly," and, "Neither could we reduce our self-centeredness much by wishing or trying on our own power. We had to have God's help."[138]

But, after accepting the guidance of a Higher Power, "As we felt new power flow in, as we enjoyed peace of mind, as we discovered we could face life successfully, as we became conscious of His presence, we began to lose our fear of today, tomorrow or the hereafter. We were reborn."[139]

---

[136] Brené Brown, "The Power of Vulnerability," *TED Talks*, TedxHouston, June 2010 (https://www.ted.com/talks/brene_brown_on_vulnerability#t-440500, accessed September 6, 2019).
[137] *Alcoholics Anonymous*, 59.
[138] Ibid., 45, 62.
[139] Ibid., 63.

Once again, we lack the ability to change ourselves, but that does not mean we are beyond hope.[140]

*   *   *   *

We live in a "pull yourself up by your own bootstraps" culture. Often we point to the early New England settlers as the source of this American ideal. But we forget that nearly half the Pilgrims died that first winter, and the remainder only survived because of help from their Wampanoag neighbors. We forget John Winthrop's insistence that the rich help the poor, and Edward Winslow's tireless efforts to negotiate peace and mutually-beneficial trade agreements with native tribes throughout the area.[141]

Self-sufficiency may work for some people. But for addicts, it means death. Like the Pilgrims facing a harsh, New England winter without the proper resources, we cannot survive without help.

Powerlessness is our admission of that painful fact. We need help. We can't escape addiction on our own.

Do we remain powerless as we recover? Yes, and no. *Alcoholics Anonymous* writes, "The alcoholic at certain times has no effective mental defense against the first drink. Except in a few rare cases, neither he nor any other human being can provide such a defense. His defense must come from a Higher Power." Later in the book, however, it

---

[140] Those who are agnostic, atheist, or members of non-theistic religions may have difficulty with the idea that this power comes from God. There are other ways to conceive of this. For example, you may not know how to fix your car when it breaks down, but that doesn't mean it can't be fixed. Buddhists may object on the grounds of Dhammapada XII.160, "One truly is the protector of oneself; who else could the protector be?" (Sometimes this is translated, "One is the savior of oneself..." But see Dhammapada VI.76 on the benefits of a teacher.

[141] Relations changed markedly under the governorship of Winslow's son, Josiah, who started King Phillip's War against his native neighbors in 1675-76.

promises, "The problem has been removed." But it emphasizes that this is the case only so long as we remain in "fit spiritual condition."[142]

Kent Dunnington, on the other hand, argues that if we drink again, we never really changed.[143] But Dunnington's claim does not hold up to experience. Many people, and not only those who struggle with addiction, are plagued by sloth, or laziness. We work hard to accomplish some goal or purpose, and once that is accomplished we slack off. Those of us who dislike housecleaning may work hard for hours or days to make our house clean. We may even keep it up for some time. But after a while, as life gets complicated, we begin to let things slide. The dishes don't get washed today because we're tired or busy. The bathroom doesn't get cleaned this week because we don't find the time.

Similarly, I could get myself into shape to run several miles. But that doesn't mean I would retain that ability if I stopped working at it. Bad weather, an injury, or a change of job could discourage me from maintaining my physical health. That doesn't mean I was never able to, but if I want to continue to have this ability, I have to continue to work at it.

The strange aspect of this with respect to addiction is that we're talking about life itself. What could be more important? Yet, especially as our lives improve in recovery, we become distracted. Priorities shift. The job, the family, and the hobbies take up more time and energy. We face problems we never had before. As one of my friends says, "I now have problems in areas where I didn't used to have areas."

Perhaps these areas represent new addictions. Surely, if we put our job before our spiritual health, that would fit Gerald May's definition of addiction as "the attachment... of

---

[142] *Alcoholics Anonymous*, 43, 85.
[143] Dunnington, 78.

desire to specific objects."[144] In that sense, Dunnington may be correct.

In practical terms, as addicts we need to work to maintain our focus on what is truly important. To put our job before our recovery makes as much sense as the punch line to the joke about the man faced with a robber who demands his money or his life: "Take my life, please. I'll need my money for my old age!"

It's been said that recovery is like riding a bicycle. If we're not pedaling, we're coasting. There's only so long we can coast before we stop altogether or start moving backward.

It is true that habituation means changing our internal disposition. But human beings are flawed creatures, and addicts are surely prime examples of that. It seems equally true that our internal disposition, if not maintained, can change in the other direction.

In practical terms, the book *Alcoholics Anonymous* puts the matter well: We are relieved of our powerlessness over drugs and alcohol, at least with respect to taking the first one, "so long as we remain in fit spiritual condition." But if we stop maintaining our recovery, relapse becomes much more likely.

---

[144] May, 24-25.

CHAPTER SEVENTEEN
WHY ADDICTION IS RISING

Kent Dunnington argues that one of the great shortcomings of our secular culture is that it *doesn't* guide us in finding meaning for life. In fact, one consequence of absolute freedom of action is that "we confront an array of mutually incompatible options with the suspicion that there exist no rational grounds for choosing among them."[145]

Psychologist Anthony Synott identifies nineteen possible frameworks of meaning for life, "Hedonism and asceticism, materialism and altruism, longevity and sensationalism, extremism, biologism, spiritualism, theism, fundamentalism, perfectionism, psychologism, narcissism, militarism, loveism, rationalism, existentialism, [and] individualism." He does not evaluate which are the most effective, or how to guide people to them.[146]

Moreover, our culture increasingly emphasizes personal comfort over any notion of common good. Ayn Rand's philosophy, for example, has influenced American conservative politicians in recent decades.[147] In a speech on

---

[145] Dunnington, 111, 108.

[146] Anthony Synott, :The meaning of Life," *Psychology Today* October 27, 2011 (https://www.psychologytoday.com/us/blog/rethinking-men/201110/the-meaning-life, accessed August 20, 2019).

[147] Max Fischer, "Ayn Rand in Modern American Politics," *Atlantic* September 15 2009 (https://www.theatlantic.com/politics/archive/2009/09/ayn-rand-in-modern-american-politics/348124/, accessed August 21, 2019); Jonathan Freedland, "The new age of Ayn Rand: how she won over Trump and Silicon Valley," *Guardian* April 10 2017

economics, she dismissed the idea that people should put the needs of others ahead of their own desires.

> Now there is one word—a single word—which can blast the morality of altruism out of existence and which · it cannot withstand—the word: "Why?" Why must man live for the sake of others? Why must he be a sacrificial animal? Why is that the good? There is no earthly reason for it—and, ladies and gentlemen, in the whole history of philosophy no earthly reason has ever been given.[148]

At the risk of waxing philosophically, one of the most famous philosophers, Aristotle, did indeed give reasons for altruism that were not based in religion. Some 2,500 years ago, Aristotle claimed that "the common good [the good of the whole political community] is superior to the good of a single individual."[149] The individual good is, in fact, *dependent* on the common good.

But rather than rely on philosophical arguments, there is a better way to rebut Rand's argument: It simply doesn't work.

Happiness in the U.S. is falling. Despite higher average incomes and standards of living, we rank #19 in happiness according to a 2019 United Nations study—not only behind the Scandinavian countries that dominate the Top 5, but below England, Germany, Canada, Australia, New Zealand, Israel, and even Ireland.[150] Other measures use different criteria. The Happy Planet Index, which includes poverty

(https://www.theguardian.com/books/2017/apr/10/new-age-ayn-rand-conquered-trump-white-house-silicon-valley, accessed August 21, 2019).

[148] Ayn Rand, "Faith and Force: The Destroyers of the Modern World," *Philosophy: Who Needs It* (Signet, 1982), 61.

[149] "Altruism," *Stanford Encyclopedia of Philosophy* (2016, https://plato.stanford.edu/entries/altruism/, accessed August 21, 2019), 4.1.

rates and ecological health as measures of overall happiness, ranks the United States at 108th out of 140 countries ranked.[151]

Interestingly, the drop in happiness is often blamed by sociologists on the rise of addictive behaviors.[152] However, as noted above, psychology links happiness to finding meaning in life. One of the central issues in addiction is lack of, and search for, meaning. Thus, the reverse may be true: addiction rises as happiness decreases.

Despite the overall rise in income, despite greater technological innovations and greater connectivity to others through the internet, and despite (or perhaps because of) greater freedom from organized religion and other ways in which the meaning and morals of life have been traditionally transmitted, Americans are not happy. Kent Dunnington, James K. A. Smith, and others suggest that the reason is simple: we can't answer the question, "What is it all *for?*"[153]

Consumerism tries to answer this question. We shop to become something we're not, as if owning the right thing or looking the right way will solve the interior need for meaning. Many of us, Dunnington argues, are satisfied with this distraction.[154] But research by Ann Case and Angus Deaton shows that as incomes have fallen in the white working class, deaths from drug overdose, alcoholism, and suicide have

---

[150] John F. Helliwell, et al, "Chapter 2: Changing World Happiness," *World Happiness Report 2019*, United Nations Sustainable Development Solutions Network, March 20, 2019 (https://s3.amazonaws.com/happiness-report/2019/WHR19_Ch2.pdf, accessed August 21, 2019), Table 2.7.

[151] "United States of America," Happy Planet Index (http://happyplanetindex.org/countries/united-states-of-america, accessed August 21, 2019).

[152] Jean M. Twenge, "Chapter 5: The Sad State of Happ9iness in the United States," *World Happiness Report 2019* (https://s3.amazonaws.com/happiness-report/2019/WHR19_Ch5.pdf, accessed August 21, 2019).

[153] For example Dunnington, 122; Smith, 48.

[154] Dunnington, 116-117.

risen.[155] Consumerism, the drive for more goods, no longer works when you're losing economic ground. And all demographic groups have lost ground. The top 10% of earners made 6.9 times as much as the bottom 10% in 1970. In 2016, that had increased to 8.7 times as much.[156] Since 2010, the top 1% of Americans has held more wealth than the entire middle class for the first time in history—almost a third of the total wealth of the nation.[157]

If we are taught that economic advancement will fulfill our spiritual needs, and if we no longer have access to economic advancement, and if, as I have argued, addiction is a response to spiritual need, then the decline in economic conditions would explain both the drop in happiness *and* the rise in substance addiction and its associated deaths.

*   *   *   *

This hypothesis suggests two possible approaches to reducing addiction in society, both of which address factors which predispose people to begin engaging addictive behavior. As noted above, even if a person has the biological condition of addiction or alcoholism, this doesn't impact their

---

[155] Anne Case and Angus Deaton, "Mortality and Morbidity in the 21st Century," *Brookings Papers on Economic Activity*, Spring 2017, 421-424, 428, (https://www.brookings.edu/wp-content/uploads/2017/08/casetextsp17bpea.pdf, accessed September 22, 2018). They cannot explain why these deaths are not rising in direct correlation with income loss in other demographic groups. I speculate that whites may be most invested in economic identity because of traditional but decreasing access to "the American Dream."

[156] Rakesh Kochhar and Anthony Cilluffo, "Key findings on the rise in income inequality within America's racial and ethnic groups," Pew Research Center, July 12, 2018 (https://www.pewresearch.org/fact-tank/2018/07/12/key-findings-on-the-rise-in-income-inequality-within-americas-racial-and-ethnic-groups/, accessed August 23, 2019).

[157] Isabelle V. Sawhill and Christopher Pulliam, "Six facts about wealth in the United States," Brookings, June 5, 2019 (https://www.brookings.edu/blog/up-front/2019/06/25/six-facts-about-wealth-in-the-united-states/, accessed August 23, 2019).

lives unless they actually pick up a substance. If we reduced the causes, fewer people would engage in the behaviors, and thus fewer people would be afflicted with addiction.

The first approach would be to repair broken systems. For example, we might try to fix the inequalities in our economic system. There are many who argue that this is necessary for a variety of other reasons. It would almost certainly have an impact on the rate of addiction. The more we reduce the factors that cause people to seek relief from an unsatisfactory existence, the fewer will begin using drugs in the first place.

Likewise, more effective childhood trauma diagnosis and treatment would have a great impact on addiction. At present, as SAMHSA reports, even many of those children who *are* diagnosed with trauma do not receive any treatment.[158] Healing childhood wounds *before* drugs become involved would reduce the number of victims who become addicts.

But these changes are unlikely to originate from a political system that seems to have little interest in making them. It will be up to us in our communities to identify and make available new resources for healing.

A second approach would be to address causes as individuals and communities. For example, since lack of meaning is a primary cause of addictive behavior, we can seek meaning for our own lives and teach others to seek it also. A person who finds meaning in their life tends to be more resilient, regardless of economic conditions.

Obviously we can't rely on the government to do this for us. First, it isn't legal. The very premise of our political system is separation between church and state. Any agenda that seeks to define meaning would inevitably include

---

[158] "Understanding Child Trauma," Substance Abuse and Mental Health Services Administration (https://www.samhsa.gov/child-trauma/understanding-child-trauma, accessed August 6, 2019).

religion, or something similar, which is one primary source of meaning.

Second, the government isn't interested. Consumerism supports the American economy and, since the 1950s, has come to define what it means to be a patriotic American.[159] Financial analysts panic when Americans save their money rather than spending it.[160] The government has a vested interest in consumerism as a philosophy for life.

If we are to find meaning and teach others to find meaning, this will have to come from individuals and non-governmental organizations.

Religious bodies should be well suited to this. The very premise of religion, sociologically speaking, is that it provides meaning for life. However, much American religion, and much American Christianity in particular, has replaced its traditional religious values with consumer values.[161] Bruce P. Rittenhouse of the Chicago School of Divinity writes,

> My own research on consumerism supports the conclusion that the reason Americans remain attached to a consumeristic form of life is because it performs the religious function of providing them with an answer to the existential problem of meaning.[162]

[159] "Tupperware!: The Rise of American Consumerism," *PBS* (https://www.pbs.org/wgbh/americanexperience/features/tupperware-consumer/, accessed August 26, 2019).

[160] See, for example, Seth Fiegerman, "Are Americans Saving Too Much?" *The Street* August 4, 2010 (https://www.thestreet.com/story/12806878/1/are-americans-saving-too-much.html, accessed August 26, 2019).

[161] "From Lord to Label: How consumerism undermines our faith," *Christianity Today*, July 10, 2016 (https://www.christianitytoday.com/pastors/2006/july-online-only/from-lord-to-label-how-consumerism-undermines-our-faith.html, accessed August 26, 2019).

[162] Bruce P. Rittenhouse, "Boom or Bust: Consumerism Is Still America's Religion," The Martin Marty Center for Public Understanding of Religion,

A 2018 poll of American Christians reported that more than two-thirds (69%) believe that God wants them to prosper financially.[163] The "prosperity gospel" is alive and well in America.

For religion or any other philosophical approach to provide meaning, it must move beyond the idea that money is the goal. Money may be enough for some people. But for addicts in particular, money has always been a means to an end: drugs. To leave drugs, there must be a more compelling meaning for life, one which reaches beyond ourselves and our own comfort.

As we consider working with addicts, we might honestly ask ourselves what is our own meaning for life. Do we have a sufficient replacement to offer? Without a suitable replacement, addiction remains the only effective treatment the addict knows for his or her misery.

Chicago School of Divinity, June 18, 2015 (https://divinity.uchicago.edu/sightings/boom-or-bust-consumerism-still-americas-religion, accessed August 26, 2019).

[163] Bob Smietana, "Most Churchgoers Say God Wants Them to Prosper Financially," LifeWay, July 31, 2018 (https://lifewayresearch.com/2018/07/31/most-churchgoers-say-god-wants-them-to-prosper-financially/, accessed August 26, 2019).

CHAPTER EIGHTEEN
ADDICTION AND RELIGION

My friend Nate, with whom I used to drink and use drugs, got clean and sober in a church. Years ago, when I was still an agnostic looking for God, he invited me to attend his church.

"You'll love it," he assured me. "They play rock music, and the pastor has long hair."

That was all true. The music was fun, and the pastor looked like someone I could relate to.

When the pastor got up to preach, his sermon topic was how Twelve Step programs are the tool of the Devil because they teach people they can have any higher power they want —and, of course, the pastor had one particular religious view in mind.[164]

By the time he finished his sermon, I couldn't wait for church to be over. The Twelve Steps had saved my life. If the only way I could be saved from addiction was to believe correctly, I'd have been dead long ago. I avoided church for many years after that experience.

This was religion at perhaps its most ineffective in treating addiction.

When we talk about finding meaning, religion has the potential to make great contributions. And religion does have much to offer those struggling with substance addiction. As explained earlier, addiction can be seen as a religion in the sociological sense. It provides purpose, moral framework,

---

[164] See Chapter Eight for comments on this perception of the Twelve Step programs and God.

- 155 -

identity, and a guide for daily living. In addiction, these are unhealthy and self-destructive. But the addict needs something resembling a religion to replace that negative framework within which he or she lives.

*   *   *   *

Purpose. Moral framework. Identity. Guidance for living. Every religion I have encountered, from Christianity to Buddhism, Islam and Judaism to Hinduism, offers these necessary elements. The problem with religious approaches is not that they fail to offer these, but the *way* in which they are often offered. The first thing an addict needs in recovery, after motivation and hope, is a guide for daily living.

Many of us, as we come into recovery, don't really know what we believe. Our brains are often operating at less than full capacity due to drug use and withdrawal symptoms. Any belief we might come to in that state would be childish at best.

It took me a year in recovery to admit that I really didn't believe in God. I knew I was supposed to, so I said I did. But, until I got honest, I couldn't really begin the work that makes long-term recovery possible. (I did finally come to believe in God, at 14 years clean and sober.)

Faith, and certainly mature faith, is something that comes to most of us over time. An approach that begins the recovery process with belief will fail for most addicts.

Because guidance for daily living is so important, most churches don't have what addicts need. Most churches meet weekly, not daily. An hour or so each week cannot replace the addict's daily "worship" of the drug.

On the other hand, Christianity, for example, speaks of daily discipleship. "If any want to become my followers, let them deny themselves and take up your cross *daily* and follow me" (Luke 9:23). Judaism, Buddhism, Islam, and many forms of Hinduism have comparable paths of daily devotion. This is a level of dedication most religious people don't seek. Whether or not it might help them, even make them happier, non-addicts generally don't need this daily commitment to survive.

Addicts do need this level of commitment. Their lives are at stake.

There are religious people who *do* make such a commitment. Monks, nuns, ascetics, *sunyasi*, certain religious communities, and others separate themselves from the world in order to follow their chosen religious path. But this higher level of devotion does not appeal to the majority, and addicts are no exception.

What is needed is a daily devotion that gives purpose and guidance *while* and *for* living in the world.

The Twelve Step programs offer this. Daily contact with others, daily attention to spiritual disciplines, and, at least in most larger towns and cities, access to daily meetings, create a community that really *does* provide daily focus on one's spiritual life.

Why can't a church community do this? It could, if it was inclined to. But for most churchgoers, this is more commitment than they care for.

For addicts and alcoholics, this level of commitment is essential. And this is one reason churches have so often been ineffective at helping addicts. What addicts *need* is not what congregations are prepared to *give*.

*   *   *   *

Before a congregation decides to undertake ministry in addiction, there's another factor to consider. Addicts tend to have messy lives. Often, it's the mess that motivates us to seek recovery. Beyond the initial mess, we really don't know how to live in the world apart from our addiction. When all our money supports our drug or alcohol habit, we don't learn healthy financial management. When we are outcast from society, we don't learn how to have healthy relationships. When all our friends are just as dedicated to their drug as we are to ours, with the accompanying moral code that puts acquisition of drugs first, we don't learn trust. We may also have health issues and mental health challenges. We tend to live from crisis to crisis.

Walking with people like this takes a lot of energy. Pastor Wesley Bontreger notes how difficult it is for a congregation to sustain the commitment to walk with those whose problems seem insurmountable or incomprehensible. He writes, "The amount of time and commitment needed to walk with people in follow-up care is significant..."[165] Pastor Duane Beck notes that struggling people can "drain energy" while moving "priorities toward the urgent, away from the important."[166] Most churches are not well-equipped for addicts, nor is it fair to the congregation to demand the necessary level of support.

Perhaps one of the most challenging requirements is to work with a struggling addict not as a project, but as an equal. No one likes to feel that they are different. Addicts already feel this way. An attitude that projects any form of looking down on the person being helped is likely to drive him or her away.

A decision for a congregation to work with addicts should not be made lightly. It should be intentional and discerning, having at least some understanding of the challenges that

---

[165] Wesley Bontreger, "Congregation-based deliverance ministry," in Loren L. Johns and James R. Kraybill, eds, *Even the demons submit: Continuing Jesus' ministry of deliverance*," Scottdale, PA: Herald Press, 2006, 95.
[166] Duane Beck, "Trusting Jesus when quick fixes elude us," in Johns & Kraybill, 90.

will be faced. The decision should be informed by the experience of someone who is in recovery, whose experience can effectively describe the real difficulty the congregation is likely to face. Otherwise, the results can be heartbreaking for all concerned.

One consequence of ineffective work with addicts should not be overlooked. An addict who seeks help from a church or other religious body comes with hope. If that hope fails to materialize, the addict is left with disappointment—not just with the congregation, but with religion in general and that particular religion specifically.

Pete is a good example. Over the years, several well-meaning Christians had tried to help him. But Pete's addiction, and the effects it had on his life, were more than they could handle for any length of time. For their own wellbeing, they had to let him go.

Pete felt these well-meaning people had abandoned him. He became a passionate atheist, claiming that all religion was false, and that Christians in particular were hypocrites.

As Pete's circumstances deteriorated, he finally became desperate enough to ask for help. He came in contact with a church that tried to help him. Pete experienced some immediate benefits of spiritual healing. He felt like he was part of a community for the first time in his life. He even talked about converting to Christianity.

But over a period of weeks, as Pete's immediate crisis receded, the congregation stopped paying as much attention to Pete. The daily prayer support he received at the beginning quickly faded as congregants found other priorities. Pete's religious life began to consist of one church service a week and an occasional phone conversation. When Pete asked about baptism, the pastor suggested Pete receive some teaching. But after several weeks, no one had been found to do the teaching.

Pete was a man broken by his addiction. He needed ongoing, daily support. But the church wasn't able to offer that level of support. After a few months, Pete left in disgust. He returned to his addiction and his atheism, and regularly tells others that Christians are hypocrites.

The congregation meant well. Its members tried to the best of their ability. They were handicapped by lack of understanding about addiction, as well as lack of focus and commitment. Pete's judgment of them is, in that sense, unfair. But despite their good intentions, we are left with the question: In its attempt to help Pete did the church do more good, or more harm?

*   *   *   *

If this story sounds like I'm discouraging churches from trying to help addicts, I'm not. But I am cautionary. Like a gardener trying to perform eye surgery, it is easy to do more harm than good.

Addicts can be a challenge to our energy and our patience. But they can also be a prophetic challenge to our own devotion as religious people.[167] The addict understands what it means to be a slave, and to have a lord that one *must* obey. That his or her lord is not true God, that this is a discipleship of deception and self-deception, nevertheless highlights what true discipleship to God might look like.

Working with addicts should *not* be an occasional ministry. It should be engaged in with deep discernment, awareness of the challenges and needs of the addict, and with the commitment to follow through even when the addict seems unreasonably needy. Because the truth is, especially in the beginning, addicts *are* unreasonably needy by most "normal" standards.

---

[167] Dunnington, 193.

It is important to consider whether someone in the congregation is willing to take an occasional phone call in the middle of the night, or to sit with someone in frequent times of crisis. The addict may have anger issues, or chaotic relationships. He or she may not handle their money well, and often seem on the brink of financial disaster. There may be relapses into addiction. Even theft from the collection plate is possible.

Yet the addict in stable recovery tends to be honest, committed, and spiritually mature. Such people can become valuable assets in the congregation, even becoming leaders.

Of course, Christianity, as with most other religions, teaches that we help people not because of what they might provide for us later, but simply because they suffer. We might then ask ourselves, "Are we willing to work with addicts, perhaps seeking for ourselves the same daily devotion to our religion that they need?" And if we aren't, why not?

Epilogue: How You Can Help

This book proposes that addiction is not as simple as most theories suggest. It has characteristics of a disease. It involves personal choice. It includes habitual actions. It involves a spiritual malady. But no single model encompasses the complexity of addiction as experienced by those who suffer.

A useful analogy is that addiction plays the role of a religion in the life of an addict. It provides purpose, identity, moral guidelines, and a daily plan for living. One might even describe addiction as a "cult," because it includes "beliefs or practices regarded by others as strange or sinister."[168] It also seeks to keep its adherents from leaving. Other addicts, who feel threatened by someone getting clean, will invariably (though sometimes unknowingly) try to tempt the recovering person back into addiction.

This analogy of addiction as religion or cult helps us to understand *why* addicts behave as they do, and why recovery can be so elusive. Addiction provides *order* and *purpose* for the addict's life. These are not easily found in the "real" world of secular Western society. In fact, apart from religious communities, the Twelve Steps are one of the few places one *can* find a suitable replacement.[169]

---

[168] "Cult," Google Dictionary (https://www.google.com/search?q=cult+definition&oq=cult+&aqs=chrome.2.69i57j0l4j69i60.4395j0j7&sourceid=chrome&ie=UTF-8, accessed September 4, 2019).

[169] On AA sometimes being described as a cult see Jennifer Matesa, "Is AA a cult, or a culture?" *The Fix* January 27, 2014 (https://www.thefix.com/content/aa-cult-or-culture, accessed September

This also highlights why religious congregations often fail in their efforts to help addicts. Most American religious members don't seem to need the same level of connection, contact, support, and daily structure for living that addiction offers. Thus, most congregations are not oriented toward providing the very things an addict needs in order to recover.

Many people have loved ones who suffer from addiction. In their well-intentioned efforts to help these suffering people, they are often handicapped by the mistaken belief that what they need is what addicts need.

This leads to thoughts like, "Just snap out of it and join the real world."

"Put down the pipe and get a job."

"You've got so much *potential!*"

Such thoughts miss the point: The addict is seeking something the "real" world can't provide—a purpose for life *beyond* punching a clock, watching TV, and shopping.

These misperceptions aren't helped by the addict's own denial. He or she will insist that their problem lies anywhere *but* the drug to which they are addicted. If they could just solve their problems, they could get their drug use under control.

Technically, this may be true. But the problem to be solved is not the unjust boss, the empty bank account, or the misunderstanding spouse. It is the hurt and pain they carry, and the need for healing and purpose.

Of course, no practicing addict wants to hear an answer like that. No one wants to admit how wounded and vulnerable they are, especially in the difficult world of addiction.

As we seek to help those who suffer from addiction, a better approach is to offer a new vision.

What if you could be happy without drugs?

4, 2019).

What if life felt fulfilling, and your relationships were healed?

What if, instead of just getting "well," you could feel joy like you've never known before?

Such a vision would at first seem unbelievable. The addict would want evidence that such a thing is possible. And without that evidence, they *won't* believe and change won't happen. This is one reason we most often get clean in community with other addicts in recovery. An addict in recovery can help another addict find recovery.

This returns us to the question of how a non-addict can help. And you *can* help. But that may require challenging changes to your own attitudes.

It is, of course, important to distinguish between the risky user, the substance-dependent person, and the addict who can't seem to leave it alone even after a period of separation. This book, and this chapter, address the latter category.

The first and hardest thing one can do is to acknowledge that it is difficult to understand how a person feels, and what they need, if one does not share that person's experience.

This is true, for example, with combat veterans. Unless you've been there (and I haven't), it's hard to understand what they've been through and are going through. But we can acknowledge that they are going through *something*, and that we need to find ways to be supportive without presuming that what we need for ourselves is what they need.

The same is true of addicts.

This means that the people best suited to help an addict recover are successfully recovering addicts. Steer suffering addicts to communities where people have escaped the misery of addiction. This may be a Twelve Step group, a church, a recovery program staffed by recovering addicts, or some other group. The experience of those who have been actively addicted and have recovered is essential to the recovery process.

I remember, in my first few weeks of trying to get clean, hearing speakers in Twelve Step meetings tell their stories. One got sober after his fifth car wreck. I'd never wrecked a car, so I wasn't like him. One had spent ten years in prison. My total jail time was about eight hours, mainly through luck rather than virtue, so I wasn't like him.

I began to feel like maybe I wasn't as sick as those around me who had recovered. But other days, as I heard stories of normal life marred by addiction, I felt like I was too far gone, that the program would never work for me.

One day I heard something that stopped me in my tracks. A man with multiple years of recovery said, "My drug of choice was, 'What have you got?'" *That was my story.* As I wrote previously, I would do drugs I didn't like because that was better than facing the world drug-free.

In that moment, I knew that there were people in these rooms that were like me, and that I belonged. I already knew there was hope in those rooms. Now I came to know that there was hope in those rooms *for me.*

But just because you don't share an addict's experience doesn't mean you have nothing to offer. Support and love are important. And you can increase your effectiveness by understanding addiction better.

Remember that what motivates an addict to recover is not logic, but an indefinable balance of despair and hope, and an underlying need for meaning and purpose. This means we should judge carefully when to help an addict and when not to. At times, helping an addict avoid the consequences of his or her actions may prevent that moment of despair that triggers change. It is also true that in moments of despair, addicts sometimes make destructive, even life-ending, choices.

It is equally important for the addict to be presented with hopeful alternatives to their current lifestyle. The best way to navigate these dilemmas is to become acquainted with people who are in recovery, even though none of us has sure answers for every situation.

It helps to understand what treatment is in all its different varieties. Not all approaches have the same goal. Some are satisfied simply with improvement, while others seek full recovery and total abstinence. The millions of people who have recovered through Twelve Step and other spiritual programs attest that full recovery is possible.

Perhaps most important for non-addicts who seek to help is this: Never fall into the trap of believing that the goal of recovery is to get a person off drugs. It is not. Trying to get someone off drugs will fail nearly every time.

The goal of recovery is to *replace* addiction as a way of life with a *different* way of life. And that replacement must provide meaning, structure, and moral framework at least to the degree that addiction did. Changed behavior leads to changed thinking and changed lives.

It is worth repeating that the goal of returning an addict to the ways of the world is doomed to fail. Addicts engaged in their addiction precisely because the ways of the world, as commonly practiced in our society, were insufficient for their needs.

If you are to help addicts recover, you must recognize that they need something more in life, or at least something different in life, than the typical American lifestyle. Most often, this has a spiritual, even religious, component.

The book *Alcoholics Anonymous* makes a promise that many addicts find unbelievable:

And we have ceased fighting anything or anyone, even alcohol. For by this time sanity will have returned. We will seldom be interested in liquor. If tempted, we recoil from it as from a hot flame. We react sanely and normally, and we will find that this has happened automatically [through working the Steps]. We will see that our new attitude toward liquor has been given us without any thought or effort on our part. It just comes! That is the miracle of it. We are not fighting it, neither are we avoiding temptation. We feel as though we had been placed in a position of neutrality—safe and protected... That is how we react *so long as we keep in fit spiritual condition.*[170]

Perhaps this doesn't sound unimaginable to you. But to an addict or alcoholic whose life has revolved around a substance for years or decades, this is an astounding promise. I remember the first time I heard it. It sounded too good to be true. And yet I couldn't help but hope.

Deaths of despair are rising in this country. Despair is the absence of hope. Hope saves lives.

No one, including me, has all the answers to addiction. But I hope to motivate you, the reader, to explore what resources are available to addicts in your family and your community, and to better evaluate which are successful.[171] Talk to those who run successful programs. Ask about their personal experience with addiction. Learn what they do and why they do it. Ask about their success rates, and what makes a person more or less likely to succeed. Take their

---

[170] *Alcoholics Anonymous*, 84-85, emphasis added. Note that when it says "no thought or effort on our part," it means with respect to alcohol. The focus of the Steps is not alcohol, but changing our lives and our thinking. It's been observed by many that the Steps mention alcohol only once, but mention God several times.

[171] A list of resources is included as Appendix II.

contact information so you can refer others or ask for help when the occasion arises.

Check the website of your local Alcoholics Anonymous or Narcotics Anonymous groups. They'll have links to literature and schedules of their meetings. You night even attend some open meetings to better understand what they do.[172] Watch for those who have long term recovery and talk to them after the meeting. Ask if you can contact them later.

Spend time with people in recovery. Ask about their experience. Addicts tend to be self-centered people, so you're asking about their favorite subject! Most will be happy to share with you the stories of their lives.

Above all, listen to why they used drugs and how they stopped. Don't be afraid to ask questions. Anyone who is serious about their recovery will be happy to help others understand. One of the driving forces in our lives is to help others who suffer as we did.

If you belong to a church or other religious group, bring up the topic of addiction. Discuss your various experiences dealing with people in addiction. Suggest that someone with experience speak to the congregation, and look for ways to engage with those who suffer.

As someone who has not experienced addiction, it's important to recognize your own experience is unlikely to interest a struggling addict. But, equipped with better knowledge and understanding, and with a list of people you can point to as examples and resources, you can offer a message of hope to those who suffer.

It's not enough to point out what an addict is doing wrong. There has to be some hope for change. Most addicts have tried to change, and no longer believe change is possible. They need new hope, something they haven't seen

---

[172] Open meetings allow anyone to attend, while closed meetings are limited to those who identify as members. Most meeting schedules will identify which meetings are closed and which are not.

before. If you know people in recovery, you have hope to offer. Use it!

Hope saves lives.

Appendix One: Resources

General Resources:

Substance Abuse and Mental Health Services Administration
https://www.samhsa.gov/

> This government agency provides a number of services, including research and information, a treatment facility locator, and more. Their research statistics are particularly useful. Their treatment listings do not include information on success rates.

Alcoholics Anonymous
https://www.aa.org/

> The original Twelve Step program does one thing: address alcoholism. Their website contains links to online and published literature, books, and videos, as well as connections to local AA resources, and more.

Narcotics Anonymous
https://www.na.org/

> Open to all who struggle with substance addictions, NA has general information, links to literature, and a listing of local resources in your area.

Celebrate Recovery
https://www.celebraterecovery.com/

> This Christian Twelve Step group isn't limited to substance addiction, but does use the Steps. Their website includes general information, links to literature

and other information, meeting locators, and testimonials. As with other Twelve Step groups, individual success rates improve when the person actively works the Steps.

Al-Anon Family Groups
https://al-anon.org/

This Twelve Step group supports those whose loved ones suffer from addiction.

Film: "The Anonymous People" (2013)
Available on Amazon Prime, YouTube, Vimeo, and other outlets.

From the producer: "The Anonymous People is a feature documentary film about the 23.5 million Americans living in long-term recovery from alcohol and other drug addiction. Deeply entrenched social stigma and mass participation in widely successful anonymous 12-step groups have kept recovery voices silent and faces hidden for decades. The vacuum created by this silence has been filled by sensational mass media depictions of addiction that continue to perpetuate a lurid public fascination with the dysfunctional side of what is a preventable and treatable health condition... The moving story of The Anonymous People is told through the faces and voices of the leaders, volunteers, corporate executives, and celebrities who are laying it all on the line to save the lives of others just like them. This passionate new public recovery movement is fueling a changing conversation that aims to transform public opinion, and finally shift problematic policy toward lasting recovery solutions."

Blog: Guinevere Gets Sober
http://guineveregetssober.com

> Jennifer Matesa, who works for the government agency
> SAMHSA, shares her own experience as well as scientific
> information and advice about addiction. Written primary
> for people in recovery, this blog also offers insights for
> those who have not experienced addiction.

Book: The Life Recovery Workbook: A biblical guide through
the Twelve Steps, Stephen Arterburn and David Stoop
(Tyndale Momentum, 2007)

> This workbook is intended to help people with a broad
> range of substance and behavioral addictions. It is
> Christian in approach, which may not be palatable to
> everyone. However, its essays and exercises give an
> overview of the Twelve Steps in their broadest context, as
> compared with the Anonymous programs which typically
> adapt the Steps to a particular area of focus. The book is
> reasonably priced and available at most major
> bookstores and websites.[173]

Trauma Resources:

Web Resource: Strategies for Trauma Awareness & Resilience
(STAR), Eastern Mennonite University.
https://emu.edu/cjp/star/

> STAR offers a variety of training resources and
> programs for healing trauma. It is highly
> recommended for pastors, chaplains, school

---

[173] I receive no benefit from sales of the workbook, nor do I have any
connection with its authors. I recommend it because this is the workbook
my ministry uses in its Step Studies.

counselors, and others who work with people suffering from trauma.

Book: *Trauma and the 12 Steps, Revised and Expanded: An Inclusive Guide to Enhancing Recovery*, Jamie Marich (Penguin Random House, 2020)

"Dr. Jamie Marich, an addiction and trauma clinician in recovery herself, builds necessary bridges between the 12-step's core foundations and up-to-date developments in trauma-informed care. Foregrounding the intersections of addiction, trauma, identity, and systems of oppression, Marich's approach treats the whole person--not just the addiction--to foster healing, transformation, and growth."

Book: *The Little Book of Trauma Healing: When Violence Strikes and Community is Threatened*, Carolyn Yoder (Good Books, 2005)

This small book contains much practical information about trauma and trauma healing, written for a general audience.

Article: "Coping," *In Terror's Grip: Healing the Ravages of Trauma* Bessel A. van der Kolk
http://www.traumacenter.org/products/pdf_files/terrors_grip.pdf

van der Kolk's work remains important for understanding trauma. This article offers an in-depth explanation of trauma, its workings, and its impact on the sufferer.

Local Resources:

Besides local Twelve Step groups, there are a number of resources available locally. County mental health centers are generally very good at what they do, and most offer substance addiction services. There are usually a variety of treatment centers, but keep in mind that most are operated for profit, and there is no rating system or standard for measuring success. Some are better than others, and the best people to advise you are those who have been through them—in other words, people in recovery.

Many hospitals and clinics with behavioral health services also offer substance addiction services. Doctors, therapists, and counselors can be helpful in locating these. The knowledge medical professionals themselves have about addiction varies, and many doctors feel they are expected to know everything and are not willing to admit what they don't know. Some are very knowledgeable. Some are even in recovery themselves, though for professional reasons they often don't advertise it. You may wish to broach the subject with your doctor and see if what he or she says is consistent with other reliable resources.

There are religious avenues for treatment as well, including meetings, treatment facilities, and halfway houses. These, like secular facilities, take different approaches. Ask them and their former clients about treatment methods and recovery rates. Some ministers and pastors have good experience with recovery, but in Protestant denominations they seem to be relatively few because addiction often ends careers. Catholic clergy and religious people in recovery tend to be more numerous because the Catholic Church generally treats them rather than firing them.

1. We admitted we were powerless over alcohol—that our lives had become unmanageable.

2. Came to believe that a Power greater than ourselves could restore us to sanity.

3. Made a decision to turn our will and our lives over to the care of God as we understood Him.

4. Made a searching and fearless moral inventory of ourselves.

5. Admitted to God, to ourselves, and to another human being the exact nature of our wrongs.

6. Were entirely ready to have God remove all these defects of character.

7. Humbly asked Him to remove our shortcomings.

8. Made a list of all persons we had harmed, and became willing to make amends to them all.

9. Made direct amends to such people wherever possible, except when to do so would injure them or others.

10. Continued to take personal inventory and when we were wrong promptly admitted it.

11. Sought through prayer and meditation to improve our conscious contact with God, as we understood Him, praying only for knowledge of His will for us and the power to carry that out.

12. Having had a spiritual awakening as the result of these Steps, we tried to carry this message to alcoholics, and to practice these principles in all our affairs.

Appendix Three: Healing Refuge Fellowship

The author founded and pastors Healing Refuge Fellowship, a healing community for people in recovery. Healing Refuge takes an approach that combines the Twelve Steps with Christian worship and discipleship. Its goal is to replace the "religion" of addiction with a specific alternative that embraces the healing power of the Gospel.

Aware that trauma, depression, and other challenges are often precursors for addiction, Healing Refuge focuses not on the specific problem but on the solution, which is healing of body, mind, and spirit. Our meetings focus on emotional and spiritual healing, but we also network with other healers, including doctors, psychologists, and specialists in other forms of treatment including generational healing.

We do not require that people who attend our meetings be Christian, but we are Christian ourselves and take that approach.

We are also committed to helping anyone who suffers from addiction find the resources they need to recover, whether or not the person is religious. Feel free to contact us through our website, which lists our email address, FaceBook page, and phone number.

http://www.HealingRefuge.org

About the Author

D. J. Mitchell grew up in a small town in New Hampshire. He struggled with addiction for ten years, moving to Los Angeles where he could avoid the scrutiny of his family. In 1985, his friend and using buddy Ed introduced him to a Twelve Step program. He got serious about changing his life.

His initial efforts focused on financial success, but this failed to provide meaning for his life. In 1993, he sold everything and moved to Sri Lanka where he worked as a volunteer for 18 months. Upon his return, he attended Loyola Marymount University where he graduated with a B.A. in Theological Studies.

Over the years, D.J. worked as a tax accountant, and built a business raising goats and selling artisan cheese. He also worked with a team on a peace initiative to end Sri Lanka's long civil war.

In 2016, he answered the call to ministry, attending Eastern Mennonite Seminary and completing his M.Div. He currently lives in Harrisonburg, Virginia, where he ministers to people seeking recovery.

He is also the author of several novels, including the apocalyptic *Ordinary World,* and young adult fiction *Benji's Portal.* His hard-boiled mystery *Domino Theory* is told from the perspective of an addict deep in his addiction.

D.J. speaks and teaches regularly on the topic of addiction to schools and church congregations. He is passionate about this topic, and is willing to speak or teach about it anywhere, any time.

ALSO BY D.J. MITCHELL:

Domino Theory
www.DominoTheory.com

A gritty mystery introducing amateur detective Danny McCabe. What if you woke up next to a dead man... and you didn't know if you killed him?

Danny McCabe comes to in a car parked in the desert. In the passenger seat is a dead man, shot in the temple. Danny's been in a blackout for days, but he's sure he didn't murder anyone. Or did he?

More dealers die, and evidence points to Danny. Now he's sure he's being framed. With no one left to trust, Danny must identify the conspirators on his own. And his worst enemy just might be his own mind.

A heart-pounding mystery with an intimate view of the strange and crazy world of addiction!

"The prose is crisp, the plot is well-tuned, and the portrait of a drug addict from inside his own head is shockingly real."

–Nancy Heisey, Eastern Mennonite University

For more books and updates from D.J. Mitchell,
Or to contact him, visit his website:
https://djmitchellauthor.com/

BIBLIOGRAPHY

Addictions and Recovery. "Drug and Alcohol Withdrawal." Apr 12
   2019. Accessed Aug 14, 2019.
   https://www.addictionsandrecovery.org/withdrawal.htm

Addiction-Resources.com. "What America Spends on Drug
   Addictions." 2005. Accessed Aug 14, 2019.
   https://www.addiction-treatment.com/in-depth/what-
   america-spends-on-drug-addictions/

Alcoholics Anonymous General Service Office. "SMF-132:
   Estimated Worldwide A.A. Individual and Group Membership."
   March 2019. https://www.aa.org/assets/en_US/smf-
   132_en.pdf, accessed April 23, 2020

Alcoholics Anonymous World Services. *Alcoholics Anonymous* 4th
   Edition. New York. 2001.

Alcoholics Anonymous World Services. *Twelve Steps and Twelve
   Traditions.* New York. 1952.

Alderks, Cathie E. "Trends In the Use Of Methadone,
   Buprenorphine, And Extended-Release Naltrexone at
   Substance Abuse Treatment Facilities: 2003-2015 (Update)."
   The CBHSQ Report. Aug 22 2017. Accessed Aug 14, 2019.
   https://www.samhsa.gov/data/sites/default/files/report_319
   2/ShortReport-3192.html

Alexander, Monica J., et. al. "Trends in Black and White Opioid
   Mortality in the United States 1979-2015." *Epidemiology* 29:5.
   Sep 2018. Accessed Sep 22, 2018.
   https://journals.lww.com/epidem/Fulltext/2018/09000/Tren
   ds_in_Black_and_White_Opioid_Mortality_in_the.16.aspx

American Addiction Centers. "Harm Reduction Guide." Jul 19,
   2019. Accessed Aug 22, 2019
   https://americanaddictioncenters.org/harm-reduction

American Psychological Association. "Children and Trauma: Update for Mental Health Professionals." 2008 Presidential Task Force on Posttraumatic Stress Disorder and Trauma in Children and Adolescents. Accessed Aug 6, 2019 https://www.apa.org/pi/families/resources/children-trauma-update

B., Dick. *Design for Living: The Oxford Group's Contribution to Early A.A.* San Rafael, CA. Paradise Research Publications. 1995.

Ballantine, Chalmers and Karl Steven Laforge. "Opioid dependence and addiction during opioid treatment of chronic pain." *Pain* 129(3): 235–255. Jun 2007. DOI:10.1016/j.pain.2007.03.028

Bezzant, James Stanley. "'The Groups.'" *Modern Churchman* 21 (10). 1932: 537–546. Accessed Sep 22, 2018. https://hartzler.emu.edu/login?url=https://search-ebscohost-com.hartzler.emu.edu/login.aspx?direct=true&db=lsdar&AN=ATLA0001779031&site=ehost-live&scope=site

Boddy, Jessica. "The Forces Driving Middle-Aged White People's 'Deaths of Despair.'" NPR Morning Edition. Mar 23, 2017. Accessed Sep 28, 2018. https://www.npr.org/sections/health-shots/2017/03/23/521083335/the-forces-driving-middle-aged-white-peoples-deaths-of-despair

Bose, Janaki, *et. al.* "Co-Occurring Substance Use and Mental Health Issues." Substance Abuse and Mental Health Services Administration. Accessed Aug 6, 2019. https://www.samhsa.gov/data/sites/default/files/cbhsq-reports/NSDUHFFR2017/NSDUHFFR2017.htm#mde1

Bose, Janaki, *et. al.* "Summary." *Key Substance Use and Mental Health Indicators in the United States: Results from the 2017 National Survey on Drug Use and Health.* Substance Abuse and Mental Health Services Administration. 2017. Accessed Jul 25,

2019. https://www.samhsa.gov/data/report/2017-nsduh-annual-national-report

Brown, Brené. "The Power of Vulnerability." *TED Talks.* TedxHouston. June 2010. Accessed Sep 6, 2019. https://www.ted.com/talks/brene_brown_on_vulnerability#t-440500

Case, Anne and Angus Deaton. "Mortality and Morbidity in the 21st Century." *Brookings Papers on Economic Activity.* Spring 2017. Accessed Sep 22, 2018. https://www.brookings.edu/wp-content/uploads/2017/08/casetextsp17bpea.pdf

Christianity Today. "From Lord to Label: How consumerism undermines our faith." Jul 10, 2016. Accessed Aug 26, 2019. https://www.christianitytoday.com/pastors/2006/july-online-only/from-lord-to-label-how-consumerism-undermines-our-faith.html

Dodes, Lance and Zachary Dodes. "The Psuedoscience of Alcoholics Anonymous: There's a Better Way to Treat Addiction." *Salon.* Mar 23, 2014. Accessed Aug 15, 2019. https://www.salon.com/2014/03/23/the_pseudo_science_of_alcoholics_anonymous_theres_a_better_way_to_treat_addiction/

Donofrio, Justin. "Opioids: Understanding Addiction Versus Dependence." HSS Hospital. May 2, 2018. Accessed Aug 7, 2019. https://www.hss.edu/conditions_understanding-addiction-versus-dependence.asp

Dunnington, Kent. *Addiction and Virtue: Beyond the Models of Disease and Choice.* Downers Grove, IL. Intervarsity Press. 2011.

Federal Bureau of Prisons. "Offenses." Aug 9, 2019. Accessed Aug 14, 2019. https://www.bop.gov/about/statistics/statistics_inmate_offenses.jsp

Finkelhor, David, *et al.* "Violence Crime, and Abuse Exposure in a National Sample of Children and Youth." *JAMA Pediatrics.* May 13 2013. Accessed Aug 6, 2019. http://www.unh.edu/ccrc/pdf/05-13%20PED%20childhood%20exposure%20to%20violence.pdf

Fischer, Max, "Ayn Rand in Modern American Politics." *Atlantic.* Sep 15 2009. Accessed Aug 21, 2019. https://www.theatlantic.com/politics/archive/2009/09/ayn-rand-in-modern-american-politics/348124/

Freedland, Jonathan. "The new age of Ayn Rand: how she won over Trump and Silicon Valley." *Guardian.* Apr 10 2017. Accessed Aug 21, 2019. https://www.theguardian.com/books/2017/apr/10/new-age-ayn-rand-conquered-trump-white-house-silicon-valley

Givens, Ron. "Chapter 15: Religion." William Little, ed. *Introduction to Sociology*, 1ˢᵗ Canadian Edition. Accessed Aug 17, 2019. https://opentextbc.ca/introductiontosociology/chapter/chapter-15-religion/

Glaser, Gabrielle. "The Irrationality of Alcoholics Anonymous." *Atlantic.* Feb 2015. Accessed Aug 15, 2019. https://www.theatlantic.com/magazine/archive/2015/04/the-irrationality-of-alcoholics-anonymous/386255/

Fiegerman, Seth. "Are Americans Saving Too Much?" *The Street.* Aug 4, 2010. Accessed Aug 26, 2019. https://www.thestreet.com/story/12806878/1/are-americans-saving-too-much.html

Hall-Flavin, Daniel K. "Antidepressants and Alcohol: What's the Concern?" Mayo Clinic. Accessed Aug 20, 2019. https://www.mayoclinic.org/diseases-conditions/depression/expert-answers/antidepressants-and-alcohol/faq-20058231

Happy Planet Index. "United States of America." Accessed Aug 21, 2019. http://happyplanetindex.org/countries/united-states-of-america

Harvard Health Publishing. "Alcohol Withdrawal." Apr 2019. Accessed Aug 14, 2019. https://www.health.harvard.edu/a_to_z/alcohol-withdrawal-a-to-z

Healthline. "Going Through Methadone Withdrawal." Accessed Aug 14, 2019. https://www.healthline.com/health/going-through-methadone-withdrawal#takeaway

Helliwell, John F., *et. al.* "Chapter 2: Changing World Happiness." *World Happiness Report 2019*. United Nations Sustainable Development Solutions Network. Mar 20, 2019. Accessed Aug 21, 2019. https://s3.amazonaws.com/happiness-report/2019/WHR19_Ch2.pdf

Herdt, Jennifer A. *Putting On Virtue: The Legacy of the Splendid Vices*. Chicago: University of Chicago Press, 2008

Johns, Loren L. and James R. Kraybill, eds. *Even the demons submit: Continuing Jesus' ministry of deliverance*. Scottdale, PA. Herald Press. 2006.

Jones, Robert Alun. *Emile Durkheim: An Introduction to Four Major Works*. Beverly Hills, CA. Sage Publications, Inc. 1986.

Kaskutas, Lee Ann. "Alcoholics Anonymous Effectiveness: Faith Meets Science." *J Addict Dis.* 2009; 28(2): 145–157. doi: 10.1080/10550880902772464. Accessed Aug 14, 2019. https://www.ncbi.nlm.nih.gov/pmc/articles/PMC2746426/

Kochhar, Rakesh and Anthony Cilluffo. "Key findings on the rise in income inequality within America's racial and ethnic groups." Pew Research Center. Jul 12, 2018. Accessed Aug 23, 2019. https://www.pewresearch.org/fact-tank/2018/07/12/key-findings-on-the-rise-in-income-inequality-within-americas-racial-and-ethnic-groups/

Lipari, Rachel N., Eunice Park-Lee, and Struther Van Horn. "America's Need For and Receipt Of Substance Abuse Treatment in 2015." *The CBHSQ Report*. SAMHSA. Sep 16 2016. Accessed August 15, 2019. https://www.samhsa.gov/data/sites/default/files/report_271 6/ShortReport-2716.html

Lipari, Rachel N. and Struther L. Van Horn. "Trends in Substance Abuse Disorders among Adults Aged 18 or Older." *The CBHSQ Report*. SAMHSA. Jun 29 2017. Accessed August 15, 2019. https://www.samhsa.gov/data/sites/default/files/report_279 0/ShortReport-2790.html

Marion, Ira J. "Methadone Treatment at Forty." *Sci Pract Perspect*. Dec2005; 3(1): 25–31. Accessed Aug 18, 2019. https://www.ncbi.nlm.nih.gov/pmc/articles/PMC2851029/

Matesa, Jennifer. "Is AA a cult, or a culture?" *The Fix*. Jan 27, 2014. Accessed Sep 4, 2019. https://www.thefix.com/content/aa-cult-or-culture

_____. "Is It Easy to Quit Suboxone?" Guinevere Gets Sober. Apr 22, 2019. Accessed August 22, 2019. http://guineveregetssober.com/how-hard-is-it-to-quit-suboxone/#more-4397

May, Gerald G. *Addiction & Grace: Love and Spirituality in the Healing of Addictions*. New York. HarperCollins. 1988.

Meara, Ellen and Richard G. Frank. "Spending on Substance Abuse Treatment: How Much is Enough?" Addiction. 2005 Sep; 100(9): 1240–1248. Doi: 10.1111/j.1360-0443.2005.01227.x. Accessed Aug 14, 2019. https://www.ncbi.nlm.nih.gov/pmc/articles/PMC1402649/

Milam, James R. and Katherine Ketcham. *Under the Influence: The Guide to the Myths and Realities of Alcoholism.* New York. Bantam Books. 1981.

National Institute on Drug Abuse. "Is Marijuana Addictive?" Jul 2019. Accessed Sep 8, 2019. https://www.drugabuse.gov/publications/research-reports/marijuana/marijuana-addictive

National Safety Council. "Drug Overdoses." Accessed Sep 22, 2018. https://injuryfacts.nsc.org/home-and-community/safety-topics/drugoverdoses/data-details/?gclid=EAIaIQobChMIxryIk-DO3QIVDK_ICh1c7gZVEAAYAiAAEgLHnvD_BwE

Nichols, Rick. *Dirty Discipleship: The Essential Nature of Recovery Ministry in Fulfilling the Great Commission.* Lynchburg, VA. Liberty University School of Divinity. 2017. Unpublished doctoral thesis.

PBS. "Tupperware!: The Rise of American Consumerism." Accessed Aug 26, 2019. https://www.pbs.org/wgbh/americanexperience/features/tupperware-consumer/

Pétursson, H. "The Benzodiazepine Withdrawal Syndrome." *Addiction.* Nov1994; 89(11):1455-9. Accessed Aug 14, 2019 (https://www.ncbi.nlm.nih.gov/pubmed/7841856,).

Portico. "DSM Criteria for Substance Abuse Disorders." *Primary Care Addiction Toolkit: Fundamentals of Addiction.* Accessed August 18, 2019. https://www.porticonetwork.ca/web/fundamentals-addiction-toolkit/introduction/dsm-critieria

Racine, Eric, Sebastian Sadler, and Alice Escande. "Free Will and the Brain Disease Model of Addiction: The Not So Seductive Allure of Neuroscience and Its Modest Impact on the Attribution of Free Will to People with an Addiction." *Front.*

Psychol. Nov 01,
2017. https://doi.org/10.3389/fpsyg.2017.01850

Rand, Ayn. "Faith and Force: The Destroyers of the Modern World."
Philosophy: Who Needs It. Signet. 1982.

Rittenhouse, Bruce P. "Boom or Bust: Consumerism Is Still
America's Religion." The Martin Marty Center for Public
Understanding of Religion. Chicago School of Divinity. Jun 18,
2015. Accessed August 26, 2019.
https://divinity.uchicago.edu/sightings/boom-or-bust-
consumerism-still-americas-religion

Rosenburg, Alana, *et. al.* "Comparing Black and White Drug
Offenders: Implications for Racial Disparities in Criminal
Justice and Reentry Policy and Programming." *J Drug Issues*
2017 47(1), 132-142. Accessed May 15, 2020.
https://www.ncbi.nlm.nih.gov/pmc/articles/PMC5614457/

Sack, David. "Are You Addicted to Unhappiness?" *Psychology
Today.* Mar 5, 2014. Accessed Aug 20, 2019.
https://www.psychologytoday.com/us/blog/where-science-
meets-the-steps/201403/are-you-addicted-unhappiness

Sawhill, Isabelle V. and Christopher Pulliam. "Six facts about
wealth in the United States." Brookings. Jun 5, 2019. Accessed
Aug 23, 2019. https://www.brookings.edu/blog/up-
front/2019/06/25/six-facts-about-wealth-in-the-united-
states/

Sawyer, Wendy and Peter Wagner. "Mass Incarceration: The Whole
Pie 2020." Prison Policy Initiative. Mar 24, 2019. Accessed Aug
14, 2019. https://www.prisonpolicy.org/reports/pie2020.html

Schroering, Caiti. "Joanna Macy, Buddhism, and Power for Social
Change." *Denison Journal of Religion* 2010:9.

Scully, Jackie Leach. "What Is a Disease?" EMBO Reports. Jul 2004. National Institute of Health. Accessed Mar 27, 2019. https://www.ncbi.nlm.nih.gov/pmc/articles/PMC1299105/

Shuckit, Marc and Briget F. Grant. "DSM-5 Criteria for Substance Use Disorders: Recommendations and Rationale." *Am J Psychiatry* 2013; 170:834–851. Accessed August 18, 2019. https://ajp.psychiatryonline.org/doi/pdf/10.1176/appi.ajp.2013.12060782

Smietana, Bob. "Most Churchgoers Say God Wants Them to Prosper Financially." LifeWay. Jul 31, 2018. Accessed August 26, 2019. https://lifewayresearch.com/2018/07/31/most-churchgoers-say-god-wants-them-to-prosper-financially/

Smith, James K. A. *You Are What You Love: The Spiritual Power of Habit.* Grand Rapids, MI. Brazos Press. 2016.

Substance Abuse and Mental Health Services Administration. "Understanding Child Trauma." Accessed August 6, 2019. https://www.samhsa.gov/child-trauma/understanding-child-trauma

Swinton, John. *Raging with Compassion: Pastoral Responses to the Problem of Evil.* Grand Rapids, MI. Wm. B. Eerdmans Publishing. 2007.

Synott, Anthony. "The meaning of Life." *Psychology Today.* Oct 27, 2011. Accessed August 20, 2019. https://www.psychologytoday.com/us/blog/rethinking-men/201110/the-meaning-life

Taite, Richard. "Can Alcoholics Ever Drink Moderately?" *Psychology Today.* Apr 8, 2014, Accessed May 15, 2020. https://www.psychologytoday.com/us/blog/ending-addiction-good/201404/can-alcoholics-ever-drink-moderately

Twenge, Jean M. "Chapter 5: The Sad State of Happiness in the United States." *World Happiness Report 2019.* Accessed August

21, 2019. https://s3.amazonaws.com/happiness-report/2019/WHR19_Ch5.pdf

van der Kolk, Bessel A. "Coping." *In Terror's Grip: Healing the Ravages of Trauma.* Accessed Aug 6, 2019. http://www.traumacenter.org/products/pdf_files/terrors_grip.pdf

Waldron, Will. "These Exalted Acres: Unlocking the Secrets of Albany Rural Cemetery." *Times Union* (Albany, NY). Accessed Aug 20, 2019. https://www.timesunion.com/albanyrural/ethacher/

WebMD. "Does Abilify Interact with other Medications?" Accessed Aug 20, 2019. https://www.webmd.com/drugs/2/drug-64439/abilify-oral/details/list-interaction-medication

World Health Organization. "Clinical Guidelines for Withdrawal Management and Treatment of Drug Dependence in Closed Settings." 2009. Accessed Sep 11, 2019. https://www.ncbi.nlm.nih.gov/books/NBK310652/

Yoder, Carolyn. *The Little Book of Trauma Healing: When Violence Strikes and Community is Threatened.* New York. Good Books. 2005.

Zika, Sheryl and Kerry Chamberlain. "On the relation between meaning in life and psychological wellbeing." *British Journal of Psychology* 83. 1992.